GOD'S POWER IN YOU

GOD'S POWER IN YOU

William Law

ɰ *Whitaker House*

All Scripture quotations are taken from the *King James Version* (KJV) of
the Bible.

GOD'S POWER IN YOU

ISBN: 0-88368-513-2
Printed in the United States of America
Copyright © 1998 by Whitaker House

Whitaker House
30 Hunt Valley Circle
New Kensington, PA 15068

Library of Congress Cataloging-in-Publication Data

Law, William, 1686–1761.
    [Spirit of love. Selections]
    God's power in you / by William Law.
        p.   cm.
    Contents: pt. 1. The spirit of love—pt. 2. The spirit of prayer.
    ISBN 0-88368-513-2 (trade paper)
    1. Spiritual life—Christianity. 2. Prayer—Christianity. I. Law, William,
1686–1761. Spirit of prayer. Selections. II. Title.
BV4500.L3362 1998
248.4—dc21   98-10097

1 2 3 4 5 6 7 8 9 10 11 12 13 / 06 05 04 03 02 01 00 99 98

Contents

Part I—The Spirit of Love

Part II—The Spirit of Eternity

Part I

The Spirit of Love

Chapter 1

What is the Spirit of Love?

Some people say there is nothing in all my writings that has affected them more than the spirit of love that breathes in the writings. They wish for nothing as much as to have a living awareness of the power, life, and religion of love. But in a discussion of this love, an objection often rises that this doctrine of pure and universal love may be too refined and abstract. However much one may like it, one cannot attain to it or overcome all that is contrary to it in one's nature. People may do what they can, but then they are only able to be admirers of that love that they cannot secure for themselves.

Such an objection will become nothing as soon as it is looked at from a right point of view. This will occur as soon as the true ground of the nature, power, and necessity of the blessed spirit of love is found.

God's Power in You

A DESIRE FOR ALL GOODNESS

Now the spirit of love originates in God's eternal will, which only desires all goodness. God considers this eternal will in His holy being before anything is brought forth by Him or out of Him. He is the one eternal, immutable God, who does not change from eternity to eternity, who can desire neither more nor less nor anything else but all the goodness that is in Himself and can come from Him. The creation of worlds or systems of creatures adds nothing to and takes nothing from this immutable God. He always was and always will be the same immutable Will for all goodness. As certainly as He is the Creator, He is the One who blesses every created thing and can give forth nothing but blessing, goodness, and happiness because He has nothing else to give. It is much more possible for the sun to give forth darkness than for God to do, or be, or give forth anything but blessing and goodness.

Now this is the basis for and origin of the spirit of love in created beings. It is and must be a desire for all goodness, and you do not have the spirit of love until you have this desire for all goodness at all times and on all occasions. You may indeed do many works of love, and delight in them, especially when they are not inconvenient to you or contradictory to your condition, mood, or circumstances in life. But the spirit of love is not in you until it is the spirit of your life, until you live freely, willingly, and universally according to it. This is because every spirit acts with freedom and universality according to what it is. It needs no command to live its own life or be what it is, no more than you need to command wrath to be wrathful. Therefore, when love is the spirit of your life, it will operate as freely and universally as any other spirit. Love will always live and work in love, not because of any particular circumstance or location, but because the spirit of love can only love, wherever it is, wherever it goes, or whatever is done to it.

Just as sparks can only fly upwards, whether it is the darkness of night or the light of day, so the spirit of love is always in the same course. This spirit knows no difference of time, place, or persons; but, whether it gives or forgives, suffers or escapes suffering, it is equally doing its own delightful work, equally blessed in and of itself. For the spirit of love, wherever it is, is its own blessing and happiness because it is the truth and reality of God in the soul. Therefore, it is in the same joy of life and is the same good to itself everywhere and on every occasion.

Do you want to know the blessing of all blessings? It is that the God of love dwells in your soul and kills every root of bitterness, which is the pain and torment of every earthly, selfish love. All wants are satisfied; all disorders of human nature are removed. Life is no longer a burden; every day is a day of peace; everything you encounter becomes a help to you, because everything you see or do is all done in the sweet, gentle element of love.

Love has no ulterior motives and desires nothing but its own enrichment, so everything is like oil to its flame. It must have what it desires, and it cannot be disappointed, because everything naturally helps it to live in its own way and to bring forth its own work. The spirit of love does not want to be rewarded, honored, or esteemed. Its only desire is to

11

propagate itself and to become the blessing and happiness of everyone who lacks it. Therefore, it meets wrath and evil and hatred and opposition with the same one will as the light meets the darkness—only to overcome any opposition with all of its blessings.

If you want to avoid wrath and ill will, or to gain the favor of anyone, you might not easily accomplish your purpose. However, if you have no desire except for all goodness, everyone you meet will be forced to assist you in your desire. The wrath of an enemy, the treachery of a friend, and every other evil only help the spirit of love to be more triumphant, to live its own life, and to find all its own blessings in a higher degree. Therefore, whether you consider perfection or happiness, it is all included in the spirit of love. This is because the infinitely perfect and happy God is entirely love, an unchangeable Will toward all goodness. Therefore, every creature must be corrupt and unhappy as far as it is led by any other will than the one will to all goodness. In this you see the foundation, the nature, and the perfection of the spirit of love.

THE ABSOLUTE NECESSITY OF THE SPIRIT OF LOVE

The necessity of this spirit is absolute and unchangeable. No one can be a child of God unless the goodness of God is in him, and he cannot have any union or communion with the goodness of God until his life is a spirit of love. This is the only band of union between God and man. Anything other than this spirit of love is only error, fiction, impurity, and corruption that has gotten into man and must be entirely separated from him before he can have the purity and holiness that alone can see God or find the divine life. Since God unchangeably desires all goodness, the divine will cannot unite or work with any human will unless it desires with Him only what is good. Here the necessity of the spirit of love is absolute. Nothing can suffice in lieu of this will. All contrivances of holiness, all forms of religious piety, signify nothing without this desire for all goodness.

Since the desire for all goodness is the whole nature of God, it must be the whole nature of every service or religion that can be acceptable to Him. For nothing serves God or worships and adores Him except what wills and works with Him. God can delight in nothing except His own will and His own Spirit, because all goodness is included in it and can be nowhere else.

Therefore, everyone who follows his own will or his own spirit forsakes the one will to all goodness, and while he does so, he has no capacity for the light and Spirit of God. The spirit of love, therefore, is such a necessity that God cannot exempt any of His created beings from it any more than He can deny Himself or act contrary to His own holy being. But since it was His desire for all goodness that brought forth the angels and the spirits of men, He can will nothing for their lives but that they should live and work and manifest that same spirit of love and goodness that brought them into being. Therefore, everything except the desire for and life of goodness is a renunciation of faith by man and is a rebellion against the whole nature of God.

There is no peace, and there can never be, for the soul of man except in the purity and perfection of his first created nature. He cannot have his purity and perfection in any other way than in and by the spirit of love. For since God who created all things is love, love is the purity, the perfection, and the blessing of all created things. No one can live in God unless he lives in love.

HOW CHRIST IS CRUCIFIED

Look at every vice, pain, and disorder in human nature; it is in itself nothing else but the spirit of man turned from the universality of love to some self-seeking or self-will in created things. Love alone, then, is the cure of every evil. Whoever lives in the purity of love has risen out of the power of evil into the freedom of the one Spirit in heaven. The schools of religion have given us very accurate definitions of every vice, whether it is covetousness, pride, wrath, or envy, and they have shown us how to think of them as conceptually distinguished from one another. The Christian has a much easier way of knowing their natures and power and what they all do in himself. No matter what you call them, or if you distinguish them with much exactness, they are all just the same thing. They all do the same evil work as the scribes, Pharisees, hypocrites, and rabble of the Jews who crucified Christ. They all did the same work, however different they were in outward names, and all vices do the same work as well.

If you want a true sense of the nature and power of pride, wrath, covetousness, and envy, such things are entirely nothing else but the murderers and crucifiers of the true Christ of God. They are not the high priests who once, many hundreds of years ago, nailed Christ's outward humanity to an outward cross, but

14

they crucify afresh the Son of God (Heb. 6:6), the holy Immanuel, who is the Christ, every time a man gives way to wrath, pride, envy, or covetousness. Every temper or passion that is contrary to the new birth of Christ and keeps the holy Immanuel from coming to life in the soul is, in the strictest sense of the words, a murderer and killer of the Lord of life. And wherever pride and envy and hatred are allowed to live, the same thing is done that was done when Christ was killed and Barabbas was saved.

Therefore, the Christ of God was not first crucified when the Jews brought Him to the cross. Adam and Eve were His first real murderers. The death that happened to them in the day that they ate of the earthly tree was the death of Christ, or the death of divine life in their souls.

CHRIST REDEEMS US THROUGH THE SPIRIT OF LOVE

Christ would never have come into the world as the second Adam to redeem it if He had not originally been the life and perfection and glory of the first Adam. He is our atonement and reconciliation with God, because we are put back in that first state of holiness through Him when He is brought to life in us. We again have Christ in us as our first father, Adam, had Him at his creation. If Christ had not been the life that was in the first Adam, Adam would have been created to be a mere child of wrath in the same impurity of nature, in the same enmity with God, and in the same need of an atoning Savior, as we are at this day.

God can have no delight or union with any man unless His well-beloved Son, the express image of

His person, is found in him. This is as true of all un-fallen men as of all fallen men. The former are re-deemed only through the life of Christ dwelling in them, and the latter want no redemption. The Word, or Son of God, is the Creator of all things, and by Him everything is made that was made (John 1:3). Therefore, everything that is good and holy in un-fallen angels comes through His living and dwelling in them, just as everything that is good and holy in redeemed man comes from Him. He is just as much the preserver, the strength, the glory, and the life of all the thrones and principalities of heaven as He is the righteousness, peace, and redemption of fallen man. This Christ has many names in Scripture, but they all mean only the following: that He alone is and can be the light and life and holiness of every creature that is holy, whether in heaven or on earth.

The wrath of nature is wherever Christ is not. This wrath is nature left to itself and its own tor-menting strength, to feel nothing in itself but the vain, restless discord of its own working. This is the sole origin of hell and every kind of curse and misery in created beings. It is nature without Christ or the spirit of love ruling over it.

Here you may observe that wrath has in itself the nature of hell, and it can have no beginning or power in any creature unless that creature has lost Christ. When Christ is everywhere, wrath and ha-tred will be nowhere. Therefore, whenever you will-ingly indulge in wrath or let your mind work in hatred, you not only work without Christ, but you also resist Him and withstand His redeeming power over you. You do in reality what those Jews did when they said, *"We will not have this man to reign*

16

over us" (Luke 19:14). Christ never was, and never can be, in any man except purely as a spirit of love.

The vanity, wrath, torment, and evil of man is solely the effect of his will having been turned from God, and this can come from nothing else. Misery and wickedness can have no other foundation or cause, for whatever wills and works with God must partake of the happiness and perfection of God. This, therefore, is a certain truth: hell and death, curse and misery, can never cease or be removed from God's creation until the wills of men and women whom He created are again what they were when they came from God. They will then be only spirits of love that desire nothing but goodness. The whole fallen creation must groan and travail in pain (Rom. 8:22), and this must be its purgatory until everything that is contrary to the divine will is entirely taken from every creature.

THE SPIRIT OF LOVE WILL PURIFY

Every son of fallen Adam is under this same necessity of striving for something that he neither is nor has. This is so for the same reason: the life of man has lost its first unity and purity and therefore must be in a working strife until all that is contrary and impure is separated from man and he finds his first state in God. Purification is what is necessary, and nothing can take its place. But man is not purified until every earthly, wrathful, sensual, selfish, partial, self-willing inclination is taken from him. He does not die to himself until he dies to these inclinations, and he is not alive in God until he is dead to them.

17

Man needs to be purified only because he has these inclinations; therefore, he does not have the purification that he needs until they are all separated from him. It is the purity and perfection of the divine nature that must be brought again into him, because in that purity and perfection he came forth from God. He could have nothing less since he was once a child of God who was to be blessed by a life in Him. No one who is impure or imperfect in his thoughts and actions can have any union with God.

You are not to think that these words, the *purity* and *perfection* of God, are too high to be used when looking at God's spirit of love, for they only mean that the will of man, as an offspring of the divine will, must want to work with the will of God. Only then can man truly stand and live in the purity and perfection of God, and whoever does not want to work with God's will is at enmity with God and cannot have any life and happiness in Him.

Now, nothing wills and works with God except the spirit of love, because nothing else works in God Himself. The Almighty brought forth all nature for this one end: that boundless love might have infinite height and depth in which to dwell and work, and that all the striving and working properties of nature can only give essence and substance, life and strength, to the invisible spirit of love. Then this spirit may come forth and manifest its blessed powers, so that men and women born in the strength and powers of nature might communicate the spirit of love and goodness and give to and receive from one another mutual delight and joy.

Anything that is below this state of love has fallen from the one life of God and the only life in which the God of love can dwell. Partiality is a temper that can only belong to men and women who have lost the power, presence, and spirit of the universal good. Those who carry the attitude of "this is mine; that is yours" can have no place in heaven, and they cannot be anywhere because heaven is lost to them. Do not think, then, that the spirit of pure, universal love, the one purity and perfection of heaven and all heavenly natures, can be carried too high or have its absolute necessity too much asserted. There are no degrees of higher or lower in this matter, for the spirit of love does not exist until it is absolutely pure and unmixed.

Chapter 2

The Needed Response
to the Spirit of Love

In the last chapter, we looked at what exactly God's spirit of love is. Since it is such an important concept when looking at man's relationship with God, and since it is sometimes thought to be difficult to grasp, it is important to review. Also in this chapter, we will look at what our response to the spirit of love should be.

All evil, all misery of every kind, is nothing else but nature left to itself and under the divided workings of its own hunger, wrath, and opposition. Therefore, there is no possibility for the natural, earthly man to escape eternal hunger, wrath, and opposition, except solely in the way taught by the Gospel: by denying and dying to self.

On the other hand, all the goodness, perfection, happiness, glory, and joy that any intelligent, divine creature can have can come from nothing else but the invisible, uncreated light and Spirit of God manifesting itself in the properties of the human life. The Spirit fills, blesses, and unites all these properties in one love and joy of life.

Again, there is no possibility of man's attaining any heavenly perfection and happiness except in the way of the Gospel, by the union of the divine and human natures, by man's being born again from above by the Word and Spirit of God. There is no possibility of any other way because there is nothing that can possibly change the first properties of life into a heavenly state except the presence and working power of the Deity united with and working in them. The *"Word was made flesh"* (John 1:14) and must be made flesh if man is to have a heavenly nature.

Now as all evil, sin, and misery have no power of working, except in the divided, contrary properties of nature, so it is certain that man has nothing to turn to, seek, or aspire after except the lost spirit of love. This is why only God can be his redeemer, because only God is love. Love can be nowhere else except in God and where God dwells and works.

FOLLOWS PRINCIPLES OF LIFE

Perhaps you are having a difficult time attaining to this purity and universality of the spirit of love. This is because you seek for it with your mind. You wish to attain it only from a rational conviction of the appropriateness and pleasantness of it. Since having a clear idea of it does not put you immediately into the real possession of it, your reason begins to waver, and you begin to think that it may be only a figment of your imagination. But this is all your own error and is as contrary to nature as trying to make your eyes do only what your hands or feet can do for you.

The spirit of love is a spirit of nature and life. All the operations of nature and life are in accordance with the working powers of nature, and every growth and degree of life can only arise in its own time and place. Nature and life do nothing accidentally or by chance, but they do everything in one uniform way. Fire, air, and light do not proceed sometimes from one thing and sometimes from another, but wherever they are, they are always born in the same manner and from the same working properties of nature. So in the same way, love has an unchangeable beginning, always proceeding from the same cause, and love cannot exist until its own true parents have brought it forth.

How unreasonable it would be to begin to doubt whether bodily strength and health were real things, or possible to be had, because you could not take possession of them by the power of your reason! Yet, this is the same thing as suspecting that the purity and perfection of love are only ideas of the mind because your reason cannot bring forth their birth in your soul. Reason has no more power of altering the life and properties of the soul than of altering the life and properties of the body. Only the purity and perfection of love can cast devils and evil spirits out of the soul; only this can say to the storm, *"Be still"* (Mark 4:39), and to the leper, *"Be thou clean"* (Matt. 8:3).

Love being born in our hearts is one of the two basic states in which we can live. Reason can no more alter any one property of life in the soul and bring it into its perfect state than it can add one inch

23

to the height of the body. The perfection of every life can only be had in the way that every flower comes to its perfection: from its own seed and root and the various degrees of change that must be gone through before the flower is found. It is strictly the same way with the perfection of the soul. All its properties of life must have their true natural birth and growth from one another. Perfection can only spring from the seeds of perfection.

Just as the seed changes into a root, the soul must change into a higher state. Like the seed of the flower, the soul on its way to heaven must pass through death into life and be blessed with the fire and light and spirit of heaven. As the seed passes through death into life, blessed by the fire and light and air of this world until it reaches its last perfection and becomes a beautiful sweet-smelling flower, so the soul reaches its perfection. To think that the soul can attain its perfection in any other way is total ignorance. The soul can only attain this perfection when its first properties are changed and exalted until the soul comes to have its flower.

THE DIVINE BIRTH OF LOVE

You can know as a certain truth that no good can come into your soul except by its being born from above, from the entrance of the Deity into the properties of your own soul. Nature must be set right; it must enter into the process of a new birth, and it must work for the production of light before the spirit of love can be born in it. For love is delight, and delight cannot arise in any soul until it is in a delightful state or one in which it must rejoice.

The Needed Response to the Spirit of Love

This is the reason why God must become man. It is because a new birth of Deity must be found in the soul, giving to nature all that it needs. Otherwise, the soul can never find itself in a delightful state and in a state in which it can work with the spirit of love. While the soul has only its natural life, it can only be in such a state as nature is in without God: mere hunger, need, opposition, and strife for it knows not what.

It is because of nature's need for the divine that what is called the wisdom, honor, honesty, and religion of the natural man often does as much hurt to himself and others as does his pride, ambition, self-love, envy, or revenge. Though some may see man's wisdom and religion as noble, these natural characteristics are subject to the same moods and tempers of such disagreeable characteristics as pride, ambition, and self-love. This is because nature is no better in one direction than in another, and it cannot be right until something supernatural has come into it.

We often accuse men, both in the church and state, of changing their principles. However, this charge is too hasty because no man ever did, or can, change his principles except with help from above. The natural man, called the *"old man"* (Rom. 6:6) in Scripture, is always the same in heart and spirit in everything he does, whatever variety of names may be given to his actions. Self can have no motive except what is selfish, whichever way it goes or whatever it does, either in the church or state. And be assured that the nature in every man, whether he is educated or uneducated, is this very self and can be nothing else until the godly life is reborn in it. There is therefore no possibility of having the spirit of love or any divine goodness from any power of nature or any working of reason. It can only be had in its own time and place, and its time and place is only where nature is overcome by the life of God brought forth in the properties of the soul.

In this way, you see the infallible truth and absolute necessity of Christian redemption. It is the most reliable thing in all nature. The Deity must become man, experience birth in the fallen nature, be united to it, and become the life of it, or else the natural man must be forever in the hell of his own hunger, anguish, opposition, and self-torment. This is so because nature can be nothing else except this variety of self-torment until the Deity is manifested and dwelling in it.

THE NEED TO DIE TO SELF

And now you see the absolute necessity of the gospel doctrine of the Cross, that is, of dying to self as the only way to life in God. This is the needed response to the spirit of love. This Cross, or dying to self, is the one moral principle that does man any good. Imagine as many rules as you will of modeling the moral behavior of man; they all do nothing because they leave nature still alive. Therefore, man's morality can only help him to hypocritically conceal his own inward evil and act as if he were not under its power.

The reason why it must be so is plain: it is because it is not possible to reform nature. Nature is unchangeable in its workings. It must always be as it is and can never be any better or worse than its own untaught workings are. It can no more change from evil to good than darkness can work itself into light. Therefore, the one work of true morality is the one doctrine of the Cross, that is, to resist and deny nature in order that a supernatural power leading to divine goodness may take possession of it and bring a new light into it.

In short, there are only two states or forms of life: the one is nature and the other is God manifested in nature. Since God and nature are both within you, you can choose to live and work with the one you want, but you absolutely must choose the one or the other. There is no standing still. Life goes on and is always bringing forth its realities, whichever way it goes. Goodness is only a sound, and virtue is a mere struggle of natural passions until the spirit of love is the breath of everything that lives and moves in the heart. For love is the one and only blessing, goodness, and God of nature. You have no true religion and you are no worshipper of the one true God unless the spirit of love that is God Himself is living and working in you.

Chapter 3

Man's Nature versus God's Goodness

This spirit of love, which I have been talking about, is the most delightful subject in the world. I am writing all this to help us rejoice in that Deity who is so worthy of adoration. His infinite being is an infinity of love and love alone, a never-beginning, never-ceasing, forever-overflowing ocean of meekness, sweetness, delight, blessing, goodness, patience, and mercy. All this is like many blessed streams breaking out of the abyss of universal love: Father, Son, and Holy Spirit, a triune infinity of love and goodness, forever giving forth nothing but the same gifts of light and love, of blessing and joy to both angels and men, whether before or after the Fall.

NATURE EXISTS TO MANIFEST THE GOODNESS OF GOD

Look at all nature, through all its height and depth, in all its variety of working powers. Nature is what it is for this one purpose: that the hidden riches, invisible powers, blessings, glory, and love of the unsearchable God may become visible, tangible, and manifest in it. Look at all the variety of creatures. They are what they are for this one purpose: that in their infinite variety, sizes, and abilities they may be like many tangible examples, living forms of the manifold riches and powers of nature. They are like many sounds and voices, preachers, and trumpets, giving glory, praise, and thanksgiving to that Deity of love who gives life to all nature and all creatures.

Every unfallen creature has its existence and power for no other reason but to manifest and rejoice in some share of the love, happiness, and goodness of the Deity. All creatures show this love to the degree that they are springing forth in the boundless height and depth of nature.

Now this is the one will and work of God in and through all creation. From eternity to eternity, He can will and intend nothing toward them, in them, or by them except the communication of various degrees of His own love, goodness, and happiness. This is done according to their state and capacity in nature. This is God's unchangeable disposition toward His creation. He can be nothing else but all goodness toward it because He can only be who He is, and He is all goodness.

GOD'S IMMUTABLE WILL FOR ALL GOODNESS

I often find myself incapable of thinking of God in any other way than as the only good, or as an eternal, unchangeable will toward all goodness. God

30

can will nothing else for all eternity, except to communicate good and blessing and happiness and perfection to every life, according to its capacity to receive it. If I had a hundred lives, I could part with them all by suffering a hundred deaths with more ease than I could give up this lovely idea of God.

Love alone was the beginning of all creation, and nothing but love encompasses the whole universe of things. The governing hand that overrules all, the watchful eye that sees through all, is nothing but omnipotent and omniscient Love using an infinity of wisdom to raise all that is fallen in nature. This same Love saves every misguided creature from the miserable works of its own hands and makes happiness and glory the perpetual inheritance of all creation. Knowing this must be quite ravishing to every man and woman who is aware of it. To think of God, of His providence, and of eternity in this way while we are in this *"valley of the shadow of death"* (Ps. 23:4) is to have a real foretaste of the blessings of the world to come.

THE TWOFOLD LIFE OF MAN

Goodness comes out of love itself, but on the other side of this goodness is wrath. To inquire about the origin of wrath is the same thing as to search into the origin of evil and sin. Wrath and evil are two words for the same thing. Man can have no beginning or awareness of wrath in himself, except by losing the living power, the living presence, and the governing operation of the Spirit of God within him. In other words, man recognizes this wrath when he loses that heavenly state of existence in

God and that influence from Him that he had at his creation.

No intelligent creature, whether angel or man, can be good and happy except by partaking of, or having in itself, a twofold life. This is why so much is said in Scripture of an inward and outward, an old and a new, man. There could be no foundation for this distinction unless every intelligent creature, including man, who was created to be good and happy, had a twofold life in him. Such a creature as man cannot possibly be capable of goodness and happiness, and he cannot possibly lose goodness and happiness or feel the least lack of them, except by his breaking the union of this twofold life in himself.

That is why so much is said in the Scriptures about the quickening, raising, and reviving of the inward, new man, about the new birth from above, about Christ being formed in us as the only redemption and salvation of the soul. This is also why the fall of Adam was said to be a death, that he died on the day of his sin though he lived so many hundreds of years after it. It was because his sin broke the union of his twofold life and put an end to the heavenly part of it. He was, therefore, left with only one life in himself, the life of this depraved, earthly world.

It is an absolute necessity that every man or woman who wants to be good and happy has this twofold life. The twofold life is the following: man, the creature, must have in himself the life of nature and the life of God, who created him. A person cannot be a creature of God and be intelligent, unless he has the life and properties of human nature. In other words, man needs to see himself as a creature of various capabilities, who has the powers of understanding, willing, and desiring. This is his creaturely life, which, by the creating power of God, he has because he is human.

The creaturely life, even with all its various powers and capabilities is only a life of various appetites, hungers, and wants, and it cannot possibly be anything else. God Himself cannot make man through man's nature to be anything else but a state of emptiness, want, and appetite. God cannot make man to be blessed and happy in and from his natural state. This is just as impossible as it would be for God to cease to be the only good. The highest life, therefore, that is still natural and creaturely can have no more than only a bare capacity for goodness and happiness. This life cannot possibly be good and happy unless the life of God dwells in it and has union with it. And this is the twofold life that needs to be united in every good and perfect and happy creature.

Here is the greatest of all demonstrations of the absolute necessity of gospel redemption and salvation, and it is all proved from the nature of created man. There can be no goodness and happiness for any intelligent creature, except in this twofold life; therefore, the union of the divine and human life, or the Son of God incarnate in man to make man once again a partaker of the divine nature, is the one possible salvation for all the sons of fallen Adam, that is, of Adam dead to or fallen from his first union with the divine life.

NATURE'S FOLLY

Any religion of nature, such as Deism, that pretends to make man good and happy without Christ, or that makes the Son of God enter into union with the human nature, is the greatest of all absurdities. It is as contrary to the nature and possibilities of salvation as mere emptiness could be its own fullness; mere hunger, its own food; and mere lack, its possession of all things. Man, without Christ or the divine life in union with him, is nothing else except mere emptiness, hunger, and lack of all that can alone make him good and happy and blessed.

God Himself, as I said, cannot make anyone to be good and happy by anything that is in his own created nature. However high and noble any created being is thought to be, the only true height and nobility he can have is a greater capacity and fitness to receive a higher union with the divine life. Also, he has a greater and more wretched misery when left to himself and his own powers, as is manifested by the hellish state of the fallen angels. Their high and exalted nature was only an enlarged capacity for the divine life, and therefore, when this life was lost, their whole created nature was nothing else but the height of rage and hellish disorder.

This is all clear proof that there can be no happiness, blessing, and goodness for any creature in heaven or on earth except by having, as the Gospel says, Jesus Christ made unto him, wisdom, righteousness, sanctification, and peace with God (1 Cor. 1:30). The reason is that goodness and happiness are absolutely inseparable from God, and they can be nowhere except in God. On the other hand, emptiness, lack, and insufficiency are absolutely inseparable from created beings. Their whole natures cannot possibly be anything else. If it is an angel in heaven or a man on earth, it is certainly filled with a mere

34

hunger and emptiness in its whole nature. And, therefore, all that we know of God and all that we know of created beings, fully prove that the life of God in union with the creaturely life, which is the gospel salvation, is the only possibility of goodness and happiness in any creature, whether in heaven or on earth.

It is also certain enough that this twofold life must have been the original state of all intelligent creatures when they all first came forth from God. No one could be brought forth by God to have only a creaturely life and be left with just that. If so, that would be creating it to be forever in misery, in need, in wrath, and in pain. This is something more un-worthy of God, and more impossible for Him to do, than to create numberless earthly animals that will be perpetually pained with hunger and thirst, with-out any possibility of finding anything to eat or to drink.

No creaturely life in itself can escape the state of need or a seeking for something that cannot be found in itself. Therefore, as surely as God is good, as surely as He would have intelligent beings live a life of goodness and happiness, so sure it is that such beings must have been blessed in their first father, Adam, with a twofold life, that is, the life of God dwelling in and united with the created life.

The necessity and certainty of this twofold life in every intelligent being who desires to be good and happy is an important matter, and I am writing all this in order to prove it. This great truth opens and asserts the certain and substantial ground of the spiritual life and shows that all salvation is merely the manifestation of the life of God in the soul. This clearly gives the solid distinction between inward holiness and all outward, creaturely practices.

All that God has done for man by any particular dispensations, whether by the law or the prophets, by the Scriptures or the ordinances of the church, are only aids to a holiness that they cannot supply in and of themselves. Such things are only suited to the death and darkness of the earthly, creaturely life, to turn man from himself, from his own workings, and to awaken in man a faith and hope, a hunger and thirst, after that first union with the Deity's life that was lost in the fall of the first father of mankind.

Chapter 4

The Need for
Perpetual Inspiration

Some may say that those who look for spiritual inspiration and direction outside the realm of nature and instead in the realm of the twofold life that I talked about in the previous chapter are fanatics. It is quite unreasonable to call those who are perpetually inspired through the twofold life fanatics, because the only true goodness or happiness that can be in any intelligent being is merely and truly the breath, the life, and the operation of God.

If goodness can only be in God; if it cannot exist separately from Him; if He can only bless and sanctify not by a creaturely gift, but by Himself becoming man's blessing and sanctification; then it is the highest degree of blindness to look for any goodness and happiness from anything except the immediate indwelling, union, and operation of God in man's life. Perpetual inspiration, therefore, is as necessary in man's nature for a life of goodness, holiness, and happiness, as the perpetual respiration of air is necessary to physical life.

The life of created beings, while they are only creaturely and possess nothing but themselves, is hell. That is, it is all pain, lack, and distress. Now, there is nothing in the nature of a created being such as man that can make the least alteration in this creaturely life; nothing can help him to be in light and love, in peace and goodness, except the union of God with him and the life of God working in him. This is because nothing but God is light and love and heavenly goodness. Therefore, when the life of God has not become the life and goodness of a man, then he cannot have the least degree of goodness in him.

INSPIRATION IS NEEDED TODAY

It is a mistake, therefore, to confine spiritual inspiration to particular times and occasions, as only being for prophets, apostles, and extraordinary messengers of God. It is most certainly a mistake to call it fanaticism when the common Christian depends on being continually led and inspired by the Spirit of God. Even though all are not called to be prophets or apostles, all are called to be holy as He who has called them is holy (Lev. 11:44), to be perfect as their heavenly father is perfect (Matt. 5:48), and to be like-minded with Christ. All Christians are to desire only as God desires, to do everything to His honor and glory, to renounce the spirit of this world, to have their conversation in heaven (Phil. 3:20), and to set their affections on things above (Col. 3:2).

Most importantly, they are to love God with all their hearts, souls, and spirits, and their neighbors as themselves (Matt. 22:37, 39).

When we look at a work as great, divine, and supernatural as that of a prophet and an apostle, then we consider that we should and can always be in this spirit of holiness. But then, to suppose that we are not and should not always be moved and led by the breath and Spirit of God within us is to suppose that there is a holiness and goodness that does not come from God, which is no better than supposing that there may be true prophets and apostles who do not receive their truth from God.

The holiness of a common Christian is not an occasional thing that begins and ends, or is only for a particular time, place, or action. Rather, it is the holiness of what is always alive and stirring in us, namely, of our thoughts, wills, desires, and holy inclinations. If, therefore, these are always alive in us, always driving or governing our lives; if we can have no holiness or goodness unless this life works in us; if we are all called to this inward holiness and goodness; then a perpetual, ever existing operation of the Spirit of God within us is absolutely necessary. We cannot be inwardly led and governed by a spirit of goodness unless we are being governed by the Spirit of God Himself. For the Spirit of God and the spirit of goodness are not two different spirits, and we cannot be said to have any more of the one than we have of the other.

Now if our thoughts, desires, and inclinations only need to be holy and good every now and then, then indeed the moving and breathing Spirit of God only needs to govern us now and then. But if our thoughts and inclinations are to be holy and good always, then the holy and good Spirit of God should always be operating as a principle of life within us.

Scripture says, *"Not that we are sufficient of ourselves to think* [a good thought]" (2 Cor. 3:5). If this is so, then we cannot be held responsible for not thinking and desiring what is good. But we need to keep in mind that there is always a supernatural power within us, ready and able to help us to the good that we cannot have from ourselves. Knowing this, we are then held responsible for not allowing this supernatural power to help us to have the good in us that, without such help, we otherwise would not have.

The difference, then, between a good and a bad man does not lie in the assumption that the one desires what is good and the other does not. But the difference lies solely in this, that the one concurs with the living, inspiring Spirit of God within him, and the other resists it and can only be liable for evil because he resists this Spirit. Therefore, as you consider what is good or bad in a man, these characteristics equally prove the perpetual indwelling and operation of the Spirit of God within a man. This is so because we can only be bad by resisting the Spirit of God, just as we can only be good by yielding to the Spirit of God, both of which equally suppose a perpetual operation of the Spirit of God within us.

PERPETUAL INSPIRATION IN THE CHURCH

The established church firmly adheres to this doctrine of the necessity of the perpetual operation of the Holy Spirit as the only source of any degree of divine light, wisdom, virtue, and goodness in the soul of man. The church earnestly desires all of her members to live in the most open profession of it and in the highest conformity to it. This perpetual operation of the Holy Spirit may then be seen in many such prayers as the following:

- O God, as much as we are not able to please You when we are without You, grant that Your Holy Spirit may in all things direct and rule our hearts.

- We pray to You, God, that Your grace may always go before and follow us, and continually inspire us for all good works.

- Grant to us, Lord, we beseech You, the spirit to think and always do such things that are right, so that we, who cannot do anything that is good without You, may be enabled by You to live according to Your will.

- Because the frailty of man without You cannot but fall, keep us always from all things hurtful, and lead us to all things profitable to our salvation.

- O God, from whom all good things come, grant to us Your humble servants that by Your holy inspiration, we may think those things that are good and may perform the same by Your merciful guidance.

Now the true ground of this doctrine of the necessity of the perpetual guidance and operation of the Holy Spirit lies in what has been said previously of the necessity of a twofold life in every person who wants to be blessed and happy. If the life of created beings, while alone or left to itself, can only be filled with need, misery, and distress; if it cannot possibly have any goodness or happiness in it until the life of God is in union with it as one life; then everything that you read in the Scriptures about the Spirit of God as the only principle of goodness opens itself to you as a most certain and blessed truth, about which you can have no doubt.

Chapter 5

The Seed of Heaven in Man

Let me say this in addition to what I have already said about the absolute necessity of a twofold life in everyone who wants to be good and happy. We may see with certainty that the Word spoken in Paradise, the Bruiser of the Serpent, the Seed of the woman, the Immanuel, the holy Jesus—for they all mean the same thing—is the only possible ground of salvation for fallen man. If the twofold life is necessary and if man cannot be restored to goodness and happiness except by the restoration of this twofold life to its first state, then there is an absolute necessity that every son of Adam should have a seed of heaven in him. This seed will then grow up into the first perfect man by the mediation of Christ. This is the one original power of salvation without which no external dispensation could have done anything toward raising the fallen state of man.

Nothing can be raised except what there was to be raised, and life cannot be given to anything except to what was capable of life. Therefore, unless there is a seed of life or a smothered spark of heaven in the soul of man that wants to grow, there can be no possibility for any dispensation of God to bring forth a birth of heaven in fallen man.

CHRIST AS A NEW BIRTH IN MAN

If Christ had not been hidden in every son of man, the faith of the first patriarchs could not have existed, and Moses and the prophets would have come in vain. This is because faith, which is a will and hunger after God, could not have begun to exist, or have had any life in man, unless there was something of the divine nature existing and hidden in man. No one can have any longing desire except a desire after his own likeness, and no one can be made to desire God unless he came from Him and had His nature.

The whole position of Christ as a mediator, from His birth to His sitting down in power at the right hand of God, was only to help man out of a life that had fallen into death and had become unaware of Him. Therefore, His power as a mediator was to manifest itself by way of a new birth. There was nothing else that could be done. Christ had no other way to proceed because life was the thing that was lost, and life must always be begun by birth. Every birth, then, must and can only come from its own seed.

If Christ is to raise a new life like His own in every man, then every man must originally have had a seed of Christ, or Christ as a seed of heaven, in the inmost spirit of his life. This seed had to have been lying there as in a state of insensibility or death, out of which it could not arise except by the power of Christ as a mediator. Christ as a mediator is the Second Adam who is needed to regenerate that birth of His own life, which was lost in all the natural sons of the first Adam. But unless there was this seed of Christ, or spark of heaven, hidden in the soul, man could not have been saved, and Christ could not have come as our mediator.

For who could begin to deny self if there was not something in man that was different from self? Who could begin to have hope and faith and desire for a heavenly life if there was not something of heaven hidden in his soul? This piece of heaven in man's soul is lying there in a state of inactivity and death until it is raised by the mediation of Christ into its first perfection of life and set again in its true dominion over flesh and blood.

THE MYSTERY OF THE INWARD LIFE

The Ten Commandments, when written by God on tables of stone and given to man, did not then begin to belong to man. They had their existence in man ever since man was created. They were born with him, and they lay like a seed of goodness hidden in the form of his soul. They were altogether inseparable from it before they were shown to man on tables of stone. And when they were shown to man on tables of stone, they were only an outward imitation of what was inwardly in man, though what was inward was not legible because of the impurity of flesh

and blood in which they were drowned and swallowed up. The earthly nature had overcome the divinity that was in man, and it gave commandments
of its own to man. This nature required obedience to
all the lusts of the flesh, the lust of the eyes, and the
pride of life. Therefore, it became necessary that
God should provide an outward knowledge of such
commandments that had become inwardly unknown,
unfelt, and shut up in death in the soul.

But now, if all that is in these commandments
had not really and previously been in the soul as its
own nature, the tables of stone would have been
given to man in vain. All outward writing or teaching of the commandments would then have been as
useless as instructions given to stones. Now, I hope
you can conceive how all that is good and holy in the
commandments lay hidden as an unfelt, inactive
power, or as a seed of goodness, until it was called
into awareness and stirred by laws written on tables
of stone. This example, then, may help you to conceive and believe how Christ, as a seed of life and the
power of salvation, lies in the soul as its unknown,
hidden treasure until it is awakened and called forth
into life by the holy Jesus.

MAN'S ORIGINAL HEAVENLY STATE

*"Thou shalt love the Lord thy God with all thy
heart, and with all thy soul, and with all thy
strength...and thy neighbor as thyself"* (Luke 10:27).
Now these two precepts, given by the written Word
of God, are an absolute demonstration of the original
perfection of man. They are also a full and invincible
proof that the same original perfection is not quite

annihilated but lies in him as a hidden, suppressed seed of goodness, capable of being raised to its first perfection. If this divine unity, purity, and perfection of love toward God and man had not been man's first natural state of life, it could have nothing to do with his present state. If any other nature, measure, or kind of love had begun when he was first created, he could only have been called to that. No one can have a call to be above, or act above, his or her own nature.

Therefore, as surely as man is called to this unity, purity, and perfection of love, it was his first natural, heavenly state and still has its seed or remains within him as his only power of rising to that again. And therefore, all that man is called to—every degree of a new and perfect life, every future exaltation and glory he is to have from the mediation of Christ—is a full proof that the same perfection was originally his natural state and is still in him as a seed or the remains of a prior existence that will allow a perfect renewal to enter in.

And this is why you are to conceive of the holy Jesus, or the Word of God, as the hidden treasure of every human soul, born as a seed of the Word in the birth of the soul, enclosed under flesh and blood until it rises as a daystar in our hearts and changes the son of an earthly Adam into a son of God.

And if the Word and Spirit of God were not in us all as a real seed of life before any dispensation or written Word of God, we could be no more ready for the gospel redemption than the animals of this world that have nothing of heaven in them. If things such as calling us to love God with all our hearts, putting on Christ, and walking according to the Spirit, did not have their real nature and root within us, they would be as absurd and useless as making rules and orders as to how our eyes should smell and taste or our ears should see.

NATURE'S WITNESS TO AN INWARD LIFE

Now this inward life hidden in man as his most precious treasure, as the ground of all that can be great or good in him, is a mystery. This inward life has been hidden only since man's fall, and it can only be opened and brought forth in its first glory by Him to whom all power in heaven and on earth is given. And this inward life is a truth to which almost everything in nature bears full witness. Look wherever you will; nothing appears or works outwardly in any creature except what is done from its own inward, invisible spirit. This is not a spirit brought into it. It is the creature's own inward spirit that is an inward, invisible mystery until it is made known or brought forth by outward appearances.

The sun gives growth to everything that grows on the earth and life to everything that lives upon it. The sun does not do this by giving or imparting a life from outside itself, but only by stirring up growth and life in every living thing that lies as in a seed or state of death until helped to come out of it. This sun, as an emblem of the Redeemer of the spiritual world, helps every earthly thing out of its own death into its own highest state of life.

What we call our senses—seeing, hearing, feeling, tasting, and smelling—are not things brought into us from outside us or given to us by any external causes. They are, instead, the many inborn, secret states of the soul that lie in their hidden state until they are occasionally awakened and brought forth into awareness by outward occurrences. And if they were not previously in the soul as states and forms of its own life, no outward objects could bring the soul into an awareness of them. Nothing can have or be in any state of sensation except what it is and has from itself, as its own birth. This is as certain as a circle having only its own roundness.

When a person smells a foul smell, this gives nothing new to the soul and does not bring anything into the senses except what was there before. A bad smell only has the power to awaken and stir up the state of the soul that lay dormant before and that, when brought into contact with the senses, is called the sensation of bad smell. And something that smells nice likewise has only the same power, which is a capacity to stir up the state of sensation in the soul that is called delightful smell. But both of these sensations are only internal states of the soul that appear or disappear, are found or not found, whenever occasions bring them into contact with the senses.

Again, the greatest artist in music can add no sound to his instrument or make it give forth any other melody, except what lies silently hidden in it as its own inward state.

THE OUTWARD REVEALS THE INWARD

Look now at whatever you want to, whether it is animate or inanimate: everything that it is and has, it is and has because of its own inward state. All outward things can do no more to it than the hand does to the instrument, which is to make it show forth its own inward state, either of harmony or discord.

It is the same with us. There is not a spark of joy, of wrath, of envy, of love, or of grief that can possibly enter into us from outside of us, or be put in us by any outward thing. This is as impossible as it is for the sound of metals to be put into a lump of clay. And just as no metal can possibly give forth any other or higher sound than what is enclosed within it, so we, however struck, can give forth no other or higher sound either of love, hatred, wrath, etc., than that very degree that previously lay shut up within us.

Our natural inclinations have a variety of covers under which they lie concealed at times, both from ourselves and others. But when some accident happens to displace a certain cover, what lies hidden under it will break forth. Then we vainly think that some particular outward occasion has not shown us how we are within, but has only infused or put into us wrath, grief, or envy, which is not our natural state or is not from our own inward state.

But this is mere blindness and self-deceit, for it is impossible for the mind to have any grief, wrath, or joy, except what it has from its own inward state. This is the same as an instrument giving forth any other harmony or discord except what is within itself. Persons, things, and outward occurrences may strike our instruments improperly and variously, but whatever we are in ourselves is what our outward sound will be, whatever happens to strike us.

If our inward state is the renewed life of Christ within us, then everything and every occasion, whatever it may be, will only make the same renewed life

50

to come forth and show itself. Then, if one cheek is smitten, we may meekly turn the other also. But if unrenewed nature is alive in us and only under a religious cover, then every outward accident that shakes or disturbs this cover will allow that bad state that lies hidden within us, whether of grief, wrath, or joy, to show itself. But nothing at any time makes the least outward show or sound, except only what is already within us to be outwardly shown, as occasion should offer.

Therefore, what a miserable mistake it is to place religious goodness in outward observances and in notions and opinions that good and bad men can equally receive and practice. It is also a mistake to treat the ready, real power and operation of the inward life of God in our souls as fanaticism, when not only the whole letter and spirit of Scripture, but also every operation in nature and creation demonstrates that the kingdom of heaven must be all within us, or it never can possibly belong to us. Goodness, piety, and holiness can only be ours, as thinking, willing, and desiring are ours, by being in us as a power of heaven in our own lives.

THE WAY OF SALVATION

Seeing that the inward life of Christ is the only real operation of heaven in man, the only work of Christ as your redeemer is the following: to take from the earthly life of flesh and blood its usurped power and to raise the smothered spark of heaven out of its state of death into a powerful, governing life of the whole man. Because of this, your only work under your Redeemer is also fully known. You

have the utmost certainty of what you are to do,
where you are to seek, and in what you are to find
your salvation.

What You Are to Do

All that you have to do is to oppose, resist, and,
as far as you can, renounce the evil inclinations and
workings of your own earthly nature. You are under
the power of no other enemy, are held in no other
captivity, and need no other deliverance except from
the power of your own earthly self. This is the one
murderer of the divine life within you. It is your own
Cain that murders your own Abel. Everything that
your earthly nature does is under the influence of
self-will, self-love, and self-seeking, whether it carries you to laudable or blamable practices. All is
done in the nature and spirit of Cain and only helps
you to the sort of "goodness" that Cain had when he
killed his brother. For every action and motion of
self has the spirit of anti-Christ and murders the divine life within you.

Therefore, do not judge yourself by considering
how many things you do that are called virtue and
goodness by those who are considered divine and
moral, or how much you abstain from those things
that are called sin and vice by the same people. But,
instead, daily and hourly, in every step that you
take, see if the spirit within you, which guides you, is
of heaven or of earth. And consider everything in
which your earthly nature, your own love, and your
self-seeking has any share in you to be sin and Satan. Do not think that any goodness is brought to
life in you except as far as it is an actual death to

pride, vanity, wrath, and the selfish inclinations of your fallen, earthly life.

Where You Are to Seek

You do not seek your salvation by taking up your walking stick or crossing the seas to find out a new Luther or a new Calvin in order to clothe yourself with their opinions. You will always feel at home with the oracle that seems to speak the truth to you because nothing is your truth except the good and evil that is yours within you. Salvation or damnation is no outward thing that is brought into you from outside of you, but it is only what springs up within you as the birth and state of your own life. What you are in yourself is all that can be either your salvation or damnation.

All that is our good and all that is our bad has no place or power except within us. Again, nothing that we do is bad except for this reason: because it resists the power and working of God within us. Nothing that we do can be good unless it conforms to the Spirit of God within us. And therefore, as all that can be good and all that can be evil in you necessarily supposes a God working within you, you have the utmost certainty that God, salvation, and the kingdom of heaven are nowhere to be sought or found except within you.

All outward religion from the fall of man to this day is not for itself, but is merely for the sake of an inward and divine life that was lost when Adam died his first death in Paradise. Therefore, it may well be said that *"circumcision is nothing, and uncircumcision is nothing"* (1 Cor. 7:19), because nothing outward is needed. And, in addition, nothing can be available but the new creature called out of its captivity under the death and darkness of flesh and blood into the light, life, and perfection of its first creation.

In What You Are to Find Salvation

In this you also have the fullest proof of what your salvation precisely is comprised: not any historic faith, or knowledge of anything absent or distant from you; not any variety of restraints, rules, and methods of practicing virtues; not any formality of opinion about faith and works, repentance, forgiveness of sins, or justification and sanctification; and not any truth or righteousness that you can have from yourself, from the best of men or books. But, you can find your salvation wholly and solely in the life of God, or Christ, awakened and born again in you, or in other words, in the restoration and perfect union of the first twofold life in humanity.

THE KINGDOM OF HEAVEN

Once the way to salvation is discovered and followed, the kingdom of heaven will be in your reach. God's kingdom of heaven is the eternal nature we receive from Him. Eternal nature has often been so spoken of: as surely as there is an eternal God, so sure it is that there is an eternal nature as universal, as unlimited, as God Himself. This eternal nature works everywhere God is, and therefore exists everywhere equally as His kingdom of heaven or the outward manifestation of the invisible riches, powers, and glories of the Deity.

The Seed of Heaven in Man

And this is eternal nature or the manifestation of the Deity, called the kingdom of heaven—in other words, an infinity, or a boundless opening of the properties, powers, wonders, and glories of the hidden Deity. This is not done once, but it is ever occurring, ever standing in the same point of action, forever and ever breaking forth and springing up in new forms and openings of the unfathomable Deity in the powers of nature. And out of this ocean of manifested powers of nature, the will of the Deity created hosts of heavenly beings, full of the heavenly wonders that were introduced into a participation of the infinity of God. These heavenly beings were created to live in an eternal succession of heavenly sensations, to see and feel, to taste and find new forms of delight in an inexhaustible source of ever changing and never ceasing wonders of the divine glory.

What an eternity this is, out of which and for which your eternal soul was created! What little insignificant things are all that an earthly ambition can set before you! Bear the rags of your earthly nature with patience for a while, the veil and darkness of flesh and blood as the lot of your inheritance from father Adam, but think nothing worth a thought except what will bring you back to your first glory and land you safely in the region of eternity.

The Deity is an infinite abundance, or fullness of riches and powers in and from itself, and only need and desire are excluded from it and can have no existence in it. Here lies the true, immutable distinction between God and nature, which shows why neither can ever be changed into the other. It is because God is a universal all, and nature or desire is a universal lack or need to be filled with God.

Now since nature can be nothing except a desire, so nothing can be done in any natural way except as desire does it, because desire is the extent of nature. And therefore, there is no strength or substance, no power or motion, no cause or effect in nature, except what is in itself a desire or the effect of it.

If nature is mere lack and has nothing in it except a burden of neediness generated from the self-tormenting properties of a desire; if God is all love, joy, and happiness, an infinite supply of all blessings; then the limits and bounds of good and evil, of happiness and misery, are made as visibly distinct and as certainly known as the difference between a circle and a straight line. When an individual lives entirely according to natural desires, he unavoidably enters into the region of all evil and misery because nature has nothing else in it. On the other hand, to die to these desires, that is, to turn from nature to God, is to be united with the infinite source of all that is good and blessed and happy.

Chapter 6

Jesus Is Our
Only Salvation

In the first several chapters, I have discussed the matter of the spirit of love. Take this matter as it truly is in itself: God is all love and goodness in Himself and therefore can be nothing else but all love and goodness toward fallen man. It is also that fallen man is subject to no pain or misery either now or in the future except what is the natural, unavoidable, essential effect of his own evil and disordered nature, which is impossible to be altered by himself.

And this matter deals with the fact that the infinite, never ceasing love of God has given Jesus Christ to be the highest and only possible means that heaven and earth can afford to save man from himself, from his own evil, misery, and death, and to restore his original divine life to him. When you look at this matter in this true light, then the God of all love and the atonement for sin by Christ, not made to pacify a wrath in God but to bring forth, fulfill, and restore righteousness in the creature that had lost it, have everything that can make the providence of God adorable and the state of man comfortable.

CHRIST'S PROCESS OF SALVATION

The Atonement of Christ is nothing else in itself except the highest, most natural and effective means that the infinite love and wisdom of God could use to put an end to sin, death, and hell and restore man's first divine state or life. I say that this is the most natural, effective means out of all the possibilities of the natural world because there is nothing that is supernatural, however mysterious, in the whole system of our redemption. Every part of it has its ground in the workings and powers of nature, and our redemption is only nature set right, or made to be what it ought to be.

There is nothing that is supernatural except God alone. Everything besides Him is from the natural world and subject to it. It can never rise out of it or have anything contrary to it. No one can have either health or sickness, good or evil, or any state either from God or itself but what he has strictly according to the capacities, powers, and workings of nature.

The mystery of our redemption, though it comes from the supernatural God, has nothing in it except what is done according to the powers of nature. There is nothing supernatural in our redemption or belonging to it except that supernatural love and wisdom that brought redemption forth, presides over it, and will direct it until Christ, as the Second Adam, has removed and extinguished all the evil that the first Adam brought into human nature. The whole purpose of Jesus Christ, from His being the inspoken Word or Bruiser of the Serpent given to Adam, to His birth, death, resurrection, and ascension into heaven, has all of its entire basis in this supernatural reason and love. This is so because nothing else in all the possibilities of nature, either in heaven or on earth, could begin, carry on, and totally bring about man's deliverance from the evil of his own fallen nature.

Thus, Christ is the one, full, sufficient atonement for the sin of the whole world because He is the only natural remedy and possible cure of all the evil that has broken forth in nature. He is the only natural life and resurrection of all that holiness and happiness that died in Adam. And seeing that Christ's redemptive purpose is given to the world from the supernatural, infinite love of God, therefore it is true what the apostle says: *"God was in Christ, reconciling the world unto himself"* (2 Cor. 5:19).

Christ in God is nothing else in His whole nature except that same, certain, and natural parent of redemption to the whole human nature. Christ is the natural parent of redemption just as falling Adam was the certain and natural parent of a miserable life to every man who is descended from him. There is one difference, though: we are born in sin from fallen Adam whether we want to be or not, but we cannot have the new birth that Christ has all power to bring forth in us unless our heart wills so.

Nothing came to us from Adam except what is according to the powers of nature. It is the same with Christ and our redemption through Him. All

His work is grounded in and proceeds according to the powers of nature or in a way of natural order to produce its effects. Everything that is found in the person, character, and condition of Christ is only there as His true and natural qualification to do all that He came to do in us and for us. That is to say, Christ was made to be exactly what He was and is— He was the Seed of life in our first fallen father; He lived as a blessing of promise in the patriarchs, prophets, and Israel of God; He was born as a man of a pure virgin; He did all that He did, whether suffering, dying, conquering, rising, or ascending into heaven, only as such things naturally and truly qualified Him to be the producer or enlivener of a divine life in us. In the same way, the state and condition of Adam qualified him to make us the slavish children of earthly, bestial flesh and blood.

CHRIST'S SUFFERINGS SAVE US

This is the sufficient doctrine of our redemption: there is nothing in God but an infinity of love and goodness toward our fallen condition; there is nothing in Christ but what could only make Him able to give, and us to receive, our full salvation from Him. But all that Christ was and did and suffered was infinitely prized and highly acceptable to God because all that Christ was and did and suffered was what gave Him full power to be a common Father of life to all who died in Adam.

If Christ had lacked anything that He was or did or suffered, He could not have stood in that relation to all mankind as Adam had done. If He had not been given to the first fallen man as a Seed of the woman, as a Light of life enlightening every man who comes into the world (John 1:9), He could not have had His seed in every man as Adam had, and He could not have been as universal a Father of life as Adam was of death. If He had not become a man born of a pure virgin in the fullness of time (Gal. 4:4), the first seed of life in every man would have lain only as a seed and would not have come to the fullness of the birth of a new man in Christ Jesus. For children can have no other state of life except what their father first had. And therefore, Christ, as the Father of a regenerated human race, had to first stand in the fullness of that human state that all His children would derive from Him.

Here we see the absolute necessity of Christ's being all that He was before He became man, a necessity arising from the nature of what He must be to save us. He could not possibly have had the relationship of a father to all mankind, or any power to be an awakener of a life of heaven in them, unless He was both God in Himself and a seed of God in all of them.

Now all that Christ was and did and suffered after He became man is out of the same necessity based upon the nature of what is needed to awaken heaven in man. He suffered on no other account except that what He came to do in and for the human nature was nothing else but a work of suffering and death.

A crooked line cannot become straight unless it has all its crookedness given up or taken from it. This is the only possible way in nature for a crooked line to lose its crookedness. Now, the sufferings and death of Christ both stand in this same kind of necessity. He was made man for our salvation; that is, He took upon Himself our fallen nature in order to bring it out of its evil, crooked state and set it again in that goodness in which it was created. There is only one way for Him to do this, just as there is only one way of making a crooked line become straight.

If Christ was to overcome the life of fallen nature, which He had taken upon Himself, then it was just as necessary that every kind of suffering and dying be a giving up or departing from the life of fallen nature as it is for the line that is to be made straight to give up and part with every kind and degree of its own crookedness. Therefore, the sufferings and death of Christ were the only possible way for Him to act contrary to and overcome all the evil that was in the fallen state of man.

Scripture tells us, *"The captain of* [our] *salvation* [was to be made] *perfect through sufferings"* (Heb. 2:10). This was the basis for His sufferings. If He had been without this basis, He could not have been perfect in Himself as the Son of Man or the Restorer of perfection in all mankind. But why is this so? Because His perfection as the Son of Man, or the Captain of human salvation, could only consist in His acting with a spirit suitable to the first created state of perfect man. In other words, Christ in His spirit had to be as much above all the good and evil of this fallen world as the first man was.

But now, He could not show that He was of this spirit, that He was under no power of fallen nature, that he lived in the perfection of the first created man, except by showing that all the good of the earthly life was renounced by Him. He also had to show that all the evil that the world, the malice of men and devils could bring upon Him could not hinder His living wholly and solely for God and doing His will on earth with the same fullness as angels do it in heaven.

If there had been any evil in all of fallen nature, whether in life, death, or hell, that had not attacked Him with all its force, He could not have been said to have overcome it. And therefore, as surely as Christ, the Son of Man, was to overcome the world, death, hell, and Satan, so sure is it that all the evils that they could possibly bring upon Him were to be felt and suffered by Him so that He could declare His perfection and prove His superiority over them. This should help to prove how a God who has all love toward fallen man must love and delight in all the sufferings of Christ that alone could enable Him as a Son of Man to undo and reverse all the evil that the first man had done to all future generations.

THE CROSS IS THE ONLY SOLUTION

There is no wrath in God, no fictitious atonement, no foolishness of debtor and creditor, no suffering in Christ for suffering's sake, but Christ suffering and dying as His same victory over death and hell when He rose from the dead and ascended into heaven. We can plainly see what the infinite merits, or the availing effectiveness and glorious power, of the sufferings and death of Christ consist of. These merits are that Christ Himself came out of the state of fallen nature and got power to give the same victory to all His brothers of the human race.

Do not therefore wonder that the Scriptures so frequently ascribe all our salvation to the sufferings and death of Christ. Do not wonder that they are continually referred to as the wounds and stripes by which we are healed (Isa. 53:5), as the blood by which we are washed from our sins (Rev. 1:5), as the price, much above gold and precious stones, by which we are bought (1 Cor. 6:20). It is because Christ, who suffered and died, conquered and overcame all the false good and the hellish evil of the fallen state of man.

Christ's resurrection from the grave and ascension into heaven, though great in themselves and necessary parts of our deliverance, were only the consequences and genuine effects of His sufferings and death. These were in themselves the reality of His conquest. All His great work was done and accomplished through them, and His resurrection and ascension were only His entering into the possession of what His sufferings and death had gained for Him.

Do not wonder, then, why all the true followers of Christ, the saints of every age, have so gloried in the cross of Christ, have imputed such great things to it, and have desired nothing as much as to be partakers of it and to live in constant union with it. It is because His sufferings and His death and cross were the fullness of His victory over all the works of the Devil. There was not an evil of flesh and blood, not a misery of life, not a chain of death, and not a power of hell and darkness that was not all baffled, broken, and overcome by the suffering and dying Christ. Therefore, the cross of Christ is the glory of Christians.

Chapter 7

Christ,
the Second Adam

The following can be asked concerning Christ's redemptive work: how it is that the sufferings and death of Christ gave Him power to become a common Father of life to all who died in Adam? Or how it is that we, by virtue of these sufferings, have victory over all the evil of our fallen state?

The fall of all mankind in Adam is no supernatural event or effect, but the natural and necessary consequence of our relation to him. If Adam at his fall into this earthly life could have absolutely overcome every power of the world, the flesh, and the Devil in the same spirit as Christ did, he would have been his own redeemer. He would have risen out of his fall and would have ascended into paradise and been the father of an offspring related to paradise. Adam would have been like Christ, when He had overcome them all, rose from the dead, and ascended into heaven. But

Adam did not do this because it was as impossible as for a beast to become an angel. If, therefore, man is to come out of his fallen state, there must be something that has power to bring it about. For it can no more be done supernaturally by anything else than it could be done by Adam.

THE SEED OF ADAM

Now the circumstances are this: the seed of all mankind was in the loins of fallen Adam. This was unalterable, and therefore all mankind must come forth in his fallen state. Man can never be in any state whatsoever, whether earthly or heavenly, except by having an earthly man or a heavenly man for his father. For mankind as such must necessarily be born of a man and have the nature of a man. This is exactly why there is so great a need for the one Mediator, the Man Christ Jesus.

Mankind must have the birth and nature that is from man. Men never could have had any relation to paradise or any possibility of partaking of it unless they had a heavenly Man for their Father; they never could have had any relation to this earthly world, or any possibility of being born earthly unless they had an earthly man for their father. Seeing that all this must be unalterably so forever, it plainly follows that there was an utter impossibility for the seed of Adam, through its own power, ever to come out of its fallen state or ever have another or better life than mankind had from Adam.

This is why there is the need for a Son of Man who had the same relation to all mankind as Adam had. This Son of Man needed to be brought into existence and was as much in all mankind as Adam was. This Son had as full a power to give a heavenly life to all the seed in Adam's loins as Adam had to bring them forth in earthly flesh and blood.

THE SEED OF CHRIST

The doctrine of our redemption absolutely asserts that the seed of Christ was sown into the first fallen father of mankind, called the Seed of the woman, the Bruiser of the Serpent, the ingrafted Word of life, called in the Gospel that *"Light, which lighteth every man that cometh into the world"* (John 1:9). Therefore, Christ was in all men in that same full relationship of a father to all mankind as the first Adam was. Secondly, Christ was born of Adam's flesh and blood, took human nature upon Him, and therefore stood as a human creature with the same relationship to mankind as Adam had. Nothing was further missing in Christ to make Him as truly a natural Father of life to all mankind as Adam was at first, except for God's appointment of Him for that purpose.

Adam could not have been the natural father of mankind unless God had created and appointed him for that end, and Christ could not have been the natural Regenerator or Redeemer of a heavenly life that was lost in all mankind unless God had appointed Him and brought Him into the world for that reason. Now the fact that God did this—Christ coming into the world by divine appointment to be the Savior, *"the resurrection, and the life"* (John 11:25) of all mankind—is a truth as evident from Scripture as the truth that Adam was the first man.

And thus it appears in the utmost degree of clarity and certainty that Christ in His single person was as fully qualified to be a common Redeemer as Adam was in his single person to be a common father of all mankind. He had his seed in all mankind as Adam had; He had human nature as Adam had; and He had the same divine appointment as Adam had. But Christ, however qualified He was to be our Redeemer, could not actually be such until He had gone through and done all that was needed for our redemption.

Adam, however qualified he was, could not be the father of a heavenly offspring until he had stood out his trial and saw himself victorious over everything that could try him. In like manner, Christ, however qualified, could not be the Redeemer of all mankind until He had also stood out His trial, had overcome all of what overcame Adam, and had set Himself triumphantly in that Paradise that Adam had lost.

Now, Adam's trial was whether or not he would keep himself in his heavenly state, above and free from all that was good and evil in this earthly world. Christ's trial was then whether or not, as a Son of Man—loaded with the infirmities of fallen Adam, sacrificed to all that the rage and malice of the world, hell, and devils could possibly do to Him—He could live and die in the midst of all these evils with His spirit contrary to them. He needed to live as much above them, as unhurt by them, as Adam should have lived in Paradise. And then it was that Christ overcame everything that had overcome Adam, and Christ's victory did open an entrance for Him and all His seed into paradise as certainly and fully as Adam's fall cast him and all his seed into the prison and captivity of this earthly, bestial world.

No Longer Heirs of the Fallen State

The fall of Adam into this world, under the power of sin, death, hell, and the Devil, enabled him to be the common father of death and to be the natural, unavoidable cause of our being born under the same captivity. Therefore, the life and sufferings and death of Christ, which declared that He broke out from them and had superiority over them, must enable Him as much to be the common Author of life. That is, His life and sufferings and death must as certainly be the full, natural, effective cause of our inheriting life from Him.

Because of what Christ was in Himself, and because of what He was in us through His whole state, character, and the divine appointment, we all had the same union with Him and dependence upon Him as our Head in the way of redemption as we had with Adam as our head in the way of our natural birth. It must be said that because Adam fell, we must all be heirs of his fallen state.

However, with the same truth and on the same ground, it must be said that because Christ our Head has risen victorious out of our fallen state, we as His members who have His seed within us must be made heirs of all His glory. In all respects, we are as strictly and as intimately connected with Him as the one Redeemer as we are to Adam as the one father of all mankind. By His sufferings and death, Christ becomes in all of us our wisdom, our righteousness, our justification, and our redemption. This is the same sober and solid truth as that Adam, by his fall, became in all of us our foolishness, our impurity, our corruption, and our death.

CHRIST PORTRAYS THE LOVE OF GOD

As we look at how Christ has defeated the fallen nature of the first Adam, we can see the glorious truth that God is mere love, which is the most glorious truth that can possess and edify the heart of man. This truth drives every evil out of the soul and gives life to every spark of goodness that can possibly be kindled in it. Everything in religion is made pleasing by being a service of love to the God of love.

God is love, and whoever has learned to live in the spirit of love has learned to live and dwell in God. Love was the beginner of all the works of God, and from eternity to eternity nothing can come from God but a variety of wonders and works of love over all nature and creation.

Chapter 8

More than Knowing

This matter of the spirit of love cannot be carried any higher in the natural sense than I have already shown. If the spirit of love were the true, natural state of a man's heart, he would leave the world as Elijah did; or like Enoch he would have it said of him that he lived wholly to love, and *"was not"* (Gen. 5:24). If there were nothing but this divine love alive in a man, his fallen flesh and blood would be in danger of being quite burnt up by it.

Even after the discussion of the previous chapter, it is possible to be in total ignorance of the true nature of the spirit of divine love. It is possible to be only charmed with the sight, or rather the sound, of it. Perhaps its real beginning is as yet unfelt in your heart. A man's natural complexion has a great deal of the animal meekness and softness of the lamb and the dove; therefore, a God of all love and a religion of all love could carry him out of all worldly cares. Then, he will be so delighted with it that he will imagine that he has nothing in him but this God and religion of love. But, bear with me if I tell you that all this is only the good part of the spirit of this bestial world in man and may be in any unregenerate man. It is so far from being a genuine fruit of divine love that if one is not careful, it may prove to be a real hindrance of the spirit of love by its appearing to be what it is not.

Maybe it would be helpful to review what I have already said about the spirit of love. It is a birth in the soul that can only come forth in its proper time and place and from its proper causes. Nothing that is brought into the soul can be taken in by any theoretical conception or delightful understanding of it. You may love it as much as you please, think it the most charming thing in the world, imagine everything else in this world to be but dross and dung in comparison to it, and yet you may have no more of its birth in you than the blind man has of light. His blindness still continues even when he has a charming idea of the light, and he is at the same distance from it, because light can only be had by a birth of itself in seeing eyes. It is the same way with the spirit of love; it is nowhere except where it rises.

THE DIFFERENCE BETWEEN KNOWING AND HAVING

I have taken so many pains to assert and establish these facts of the spirit of love because I want this spirit to be completely understood. The error that normally comes out of studying the spirit of love lies in confusing two things that are entirely distinct from each other. This error comes in making no difference between the doctrine that only sets forth the nature, excellency, and necessity of the spirit of love, and the spirit of love itself, and these things are so different that you may be quite full of the former and at the same time quite empty of the latter.

I have said everything that I could to show the truth, excellency, and necessity of the spirit of love. It is of infinite importance to be well established in the belief of this doctrine. But all that I have said of it is only to induce and encourage my reader to buy it at its own price and to give everything that can purchase it. But if you think that you have gotten it because you are so highly pleased with what you have heard of it, you only embrace the shadow instead of the substance.

The price that you must pay to obtain this spirit of love is to give up all that you are, and all that you have from fallen Adam, for all that you are and have from him is that life of flesh and blood that cannot enter into the kingdom of God.

This error of not being able to separate doctrine from the real thing can also cause one not to be able to break free from the old nature. Even though this doctrine may have gotten into someone's heart, such a person would continually be thrown out of it in practice and would find himself under the power of his old inclinations and passions as often as he was before he was so full of this doctrine.

TWO STAGES IN THE CHRISTIAN LIFE

Every kind of virtue and goodness may be brought into us by two different ways. They may be taught to us outwardly by men, by rules and precepts; they may also be inwardly born in us, as the genuine birth of our own renewed spirits. In the former way, as we learn them only from men by rules and documents of instruction, they at best only change our outward behavior and leave our hearts in their natural states. Our passions are only put under a forced restraint that will occasionally break forth in spite of the dead letter of precept and doctrine.

Now this way of learning and attaining goodness, though thus imperfect, is yet absolutely necessary and must have its time, place, and work in us. Yet this is only for a time, just as the law was a schoolmaster to the Gospel (Gal. 3:24). We must first be babes in doctrine as well as in strength before we can be men. But it must be said of all this outward instruction, whether from good men or the letter of Scripture, what the apostle said of the law: that it *"made nothing perfect"* (Heb. 7:19) and yet is highly necessary in order for perfection to come about.

The true perfection and profitableness of the holy written Word of God is fully set forth by Paul in his second letter to Timothy: *"From a child thou hast known the holy scriptures, which are able to make thee wise unto salvation through faith which is in Christ Jesus"* (2 Tim. 3:15). Now these *"holy scriptures"* were the law and the prophets, for Timothy had known no other from his youth. Like them, all other Scriptures since have had no other good in them except to lead and direct us to a salvation that is not to be had in the Scriptures themselves but from faith in Christ Jesus. Their teaching is only to teach us where to seek and to find the fountain and source of all light and knowledge.

Paul said of the law, *"the law was our schoolmaster to bring us unto Christ"* (Gal. 3:24). Peter said the same of the prophets:

More than Knowing

We have also a more sure word of prophecy;
whereunto ye do well that ye take heed, as unto
a light that shineth in a dark place, until the
day dawn, and the day star arise in your
hearts.   *(2 Pet. 1:19)*

The same thing is to be affirmed of the letter of
the New Testament; it is but our schoolmaster unto
Christ, a light like that of prophecy, to which we are
to take great heed until Christ, as the dawning of
the day, arises in our hearts. And salvation cannot
possibly be otherwise; no instruction that comes under the form of words can do more for us than mere
sounds and words can do. Such things can only direct us to something that is better than themselves,
that can be the true light, life, spirit, and power of
holiness in us.

Jesus is alone that Word of God that can be the
light, life, and salvation of fallen man. It is not possible to exalt more the letter of Scripture than by
acknowledging it to be a true, outward, verbal direction to the one and only true Light and Salvation of
man. If you had been a true disciple of John the Baptist, whose only office was to prepare the way to
Christ, how could you have more magnified his office
or declared your fidelity to him than by going from
his teaching to that of Christ, to whom he directed
you? John the Baptist was indeed a burning and a
shining light, and so are the Holy Scriptures, but *"he*
was not that Light, but was sent to bear witness of
that Light. That was the true Light, which lighteth
every man that cometh into the world" (John 1:8–9).

Now I have come to the full proof of this point,
that there are two ways of attaining knowledge,

75

goodness, virtue, and other such qualities. The one is by the ministry of outward, verbal instruction either by men or books; the other is by an inward birth of divine light, goodness, and virtue in our own renewed spirits. The former is only to lead us to the latter and is of no benefit to us except as it carries us further than itself, to be united in heart and spirit with the light and Word and Spirit of God. In the same way, John the Baptist would have been of no benefit to his disciples unless he had been their guide from himself to Christ.

From this twofold teaching, there necessarily arises a twofold state of virtue and goodness. Whatever the state of the teacher or teaching, such is the state and manner of the goodness that can be had from it. Every effect must be according to the cause that produces it. If you learn virtue and goodness only from outward means, from men or books, you may be virtuous and good according to outward forms. You may do works of humility, works of love and benevolence, use times and forms of prayer; all this virtue and goodness is suitable to this kind of teaching and may very well be gained from it. But the spirit of prayer, the spirit of love, and the spirit of humility, or of any other virtue, are only to be attained by the operation of the light and Spirit of God, not outwardly teaching but inwardly bringing forth a newborn spirit within us.

PERSONAL APPLICATION

There is much to be feared if you only stand under this outward teaching, if your good works are only done under obedience to the rules, precepts, and doctrines that your reason assents to, but are not the fruits of a newborn spirit within you. Until you are thus renewed in the spirit of your mind, your virtues are only taught practices that are grafted upon a corrupt bottom. Everything you do will be a mixture of good and bad; your humility will lead you to pride, your charity to others will give nourishment to your own self-love, and as your prayers increase, so will the opinion of your own sanctity. Until the heart is purified to the bottom and has felt the ax at the root of its evil—which cannot be done by outward instruction—everything that proceeds from it partakes of its impurity and corruption. When someone has the spirit of love really born in him from its own seed, he can account for its birth and power by knowing the price that he paid for it, and how many deaths he suffered before the spirit of love came to life.

It is good when someone confesses that his natural inclinations are not yet subdued by doctrine and precept. It is also good when one is so highly delighted with the doctrine of love. Each of these states is true preparation for further advancement. However, the same error is common to both states: persons in both states think they have as much of the spirit of love as they could have, or as they ought to have. It is therefore necessary to continue to discover the true meaning and application of the spirit of love in a person's life.

Chapter 9

The Spirit of Love
Delivers Us

W hat is divine love in itself, and what is its nature and power in the soul of man? Divine love is perfect peace and joy; it is a freedom from all disquiet; it is contentedness and mere happiness and makes everything to rejoice in itself. Love is the Christ of God. Wherever it comes, it comes as the blessing and happiness of every natural life, as the restorer of every lost perfection, a redeemer from all evil, a fulfiller of all righteousness, and a *"peace of God, which passeth all understanding"* (Phil. 4:7).

THE POWER OF DIVINE LOVE

Through all the universe, nothing is uneasy, unsatisfied, or restless, unless it is not governed by love or its nature has not yet attained the full birth of the spirit of love. When that is done, every hunger is satisfied, and all complaining, murmuring, accusing, resenting, revenging, and struggling are as totally suppressed and overcome as the coldness, thickness, and horror of darkness are by the breaking forth of the light. If you ask why the spirit of love cannot be displeased; cannot be disappointed; cannot complain, accuse, resent, or murmur; it is because divine love desires nothing except itself. It is its own good; it has all when it has itself because nothing is good except itself and its own working. Love is God, and he who dwells in God, dwells in love (1 John 4:16).

We can judge whether or not we are in the spirit of love by seeing if we have these heavenly inclinations and not by any fervor or religious desire that we find in ourselves. Just as much and as far as you are freed from the foolishness of all earthly affections, from all disquiet, trouble, and complaint about this or that, that is as much and as far as the spirit of love has come to life in you. Divine love is a new life and new nature, and it introduces you into a new world. It puts an end to all your former opinions, ideas, and desires. It opens new senses in you and makes high become low to you, and low become high; wisdom become foolishness, and foolishness become wisdom. It makes prosperity and adversity, praise and censure, to be equally nothing. Paul said, *"When I was a child, I spake as a child, I understood as a child, I thought as a child: but when I became a man, I put away childish things"* (1 Cor. 13:11).

While man is under the power of nature, governed only by worldly wisdom, his life is quite childish, however old he may be. Everything about him only awakens childish thoughts and pursuits in him. All that he sees and hears; all that he desires or fears, likes or dislikes; what he gets and what he loses; what he has and what he does not have; serve only to carry him from this false evil to that false good, from one vanity of peace to another vanity of trouble. But when divine love is born in the soul, all childish images of good and evil are done away with, and all sense of them is lost, much as the stars lose their visibility when the sun is risen.

THE POWER OF LIGHT

Now this brings us to the one great practical point on which all our proficiency in the spirit of love entirely depends, namely, that all that we are and all that we have from fallen Adam must be given up, absolutely denied, and resisted if divine love is to be brought forth in us. For all that we are by nature is fully contrary to this divine love, and it cannot be otherwise. The only cure is for self to die, and nothing else can make it subservient to good, just as darkness cannot be altered or be made better in itself or be transmuted into light. Darkness can only be subservient to the light by being lost in it and swallowed up by it.

This was the first state of man: all the natural properties of his creaturely life were hidden in God, united in God, and glorified by the life of God manifested in them, just as the nature and qualities of darkness are lost and hidden when they are enlightened and glorified by the light. But when man fell from, or died to, the divine life, all the natural properties of his creaturely life, having lost their union with God, broke forth in their own natural division, discord, and war against one another, just as the darkness must show forth its own coldness, horror, and other uncomfortable qualities when it has lost the light.

When God said, *"Let there be light"* (Gen. 1:3), and then there was light, no change happened to eternal light itself, nor did any light begin to exist. The darkness of this world then only began to receive a power or operation of the eternal light upon it, which it did not have before, or eternity then began to open some resemblance of its own glory in the dark elements and shadows of time. Thus I assert the priority and glory of light and put all darkness under its feet, and it as impossible for darkness to be anything else but light's footstool.

Scripture says that God dwells *"in the light which no man can approach unto"* (1 Tim. 6:16); therefore, Scripture teaches that light in itself is invisible to man, that it cannot be approached or made manifest to him except by something that is not light. This is all that I said when I affirmed that light cannot be manifested or have any visibility to created eyes, except in and through darkness.

Light, as it is in itself, is only in the supernatural Deity, and that is the reason why no man or any created being can come near it or have any awareness of it as it is in itself. Yet no light can come into this world except through what God dwelled in before any world was created. No light can exist in time except the light of eternity. Therefore, if the supernatural light is to manifest something of its incomprehensible glory and become in some degree tangible and visible to created beings, it must enter into nature; it must put on materiality. What is it that can be understood by the materiality of light?

Everything that can be understood when the wisdom, mercy, and goodness of God are made intelligible and credible to us by being written in ink. Light is distinct from and superior to everything by which it is brought forth, just as the wisdom, mercy, and goodness of God are distinct from and superior to everything that makes them intelligible and credible to human minds.

The incomprehensible Deity can make no outward revelation of His will, wisdom, and goodness except by articulate sounds, voices, or letters written on tables of stone or other such material things. In the same way, the invisible, inaccessible, supernatural light of God cannot make itself outwardly visible except through such darkness of materiality that is capable of receiving its illumination. The divine will, wisdom, and goodness, when making outward revelation of themselves through things that we can see and touch, are not themselves material. In the same way, the divine light appears to be material when it outwardly reveals something of its invisible, incomprehensible splendor and glory through the materiality of darkness, even though the light itself is not material.

Sight and visibility are only two powers of light, but light consists entirely of power. It is life, and every joyful sensation of life arises from it. John said of Christ, *"In him was life; and the life was the light of men"* (John 1:4). Light is all things, and nothing. It is nothing because it is supernatural; it is all things because every good power and the perfection of everything arises from it. There can be no joy or rejoicing in any created being unless it is from the power and joy of the light of God. There can be no meekness, benevolence, or goodness in angel, man, or any creature, except where light is the Lord of its life. Life itself begins no sooner than when the divine light begins it. Life rises no higher and has no other glory than where the divine light leads it. Sounds have no softness, flowers have no sweetness, plants and fruits have no growth, except what the mystery of light opens in them.

Whatever is delightful and ravishing, sublime and glorious in spirits, minds, or bodies, either in heaven or on earth, is from the power of God's supernatural light, opening its endless wonders in them. Hell has misery, horror, or distraction only because it has no communication with the supernatural light. If the supernatural light of God did not stream forth its blessings into this world through the materiality of the sun, all outward nature would be full of the horror of hell.

This is why all the mysteries and wonders of divine light in this material system are so astonishingly great and unsearchable. It is because the natural light of this world is nothing else but the power and mystery of the supernatural light of God breaking forth according to its omnipotence in all the various forms of elementary darkness that constitute this temporary world.

DARKNESS AS OPPOSED TO LIGHT

Darkness and light are the two natures that are in every man and do all that is done in him. The Scriptures only make this division: the works of darkness are sin, and they who walk in the light are the children of God. Therefore, light and darkness do everything, whether good or evil, that is done in man.

Darkness is everywhere that there is nature and creature. All nature, and all that is natural in man, is in itself nothing else but darkness, whether it is in soul or body, in heaven or on earth. Therefore, when the angels—though in heaven—had lost the supernatural light of God, they became imprisoned in the chains of their own natural darkness. If you ask why nature must be darkness, it is because nature is not God and therefore can have no light. For God and light are as inseparable as God and unity are inseparable. Everything, therefore, that is not God can be nothing else in itself but darkness, and can do nothing except what it can do according to the nature and powers of darkness. These powers of darkness are the workings of nature or self, for nature, darkness, and self are merely three different expressions for the same thing.

Now every evil, wicked, wrathful, impure, unjust thought, inclination, passion, or idea that ever stirred or moved in any creature; every misery, discontent, distress, rage, horror, and torment that ever plagued the life of fallen man or angel; are the very things that you are to understand by the powers or workings of darkness, nature, or self. For nothing is evil, wicked, or tormenting except what nature or self does.

Nature has all evil, but it has no evil in itself. Nature, as it comes forth from God, is darkness without any evil of darkness in it. It is not darkness when it is without the light and completely separate from it, and it could never have been known to have any quality of darkness if it had not lost that state of light in which it came forth from God as a manifestation of the goodness, virtues, and glories of light. Again, nature is a struggle for one purpose: so that we may become aware of the supernatural good. This supernatural good will be known, found, and felt by its taking all the evil of strife and discord from nature and becoming the union, peace, and joy of nature. The evil of strife and discord of will could never have had a name in all the natural universe if everything had continued in that same state in which it came forth from God. Nature is self, man's own life; and through such a life, the universal, incomprehensible goodness, happiness, and perfections of the Deity might be possessed as properties and qualities of life in created, finite beings. Therefore, all that is called nature, darkness, or self not only has no evil in it, but also is the only true basis for all possible good.

When the intelligent creature turns from God to self or nature, he acts unnaturally. He turns from all that makes nature to be good, and he finds nature only as it is in itself and without God. And then it so happens that nature or self has all evil in it. Nothing is to be gained from it or found in it except the work of every kind of evil, baseness, misery, and torment, and the utmost opposition to God and all goodness. And thus you also see the plainness and certainty of my assertion that nature or self has all evil and yet no evil in it.

THE TRUE NATURE OF SELF

Nature or self without God manifested in it is all evil and misery. But what is the precise nature of self, or what is it that makes it to be so full of evil and misery? Covetousness, envy, pride, and wrath are the four elements of self, nature, or hell; all of them are inseparable from it. And the reason why this must be so and cannot be otherwise is that the natural life of man is brought forth for participation in some high, supernatural good in the Creator. But it could have no fitness or possible capacity to receive such good unless it was in itself both an extreme need and an extreme desire for some high good. When, therefore, this natural life is deprived of or fallen from God, it can be nothing else in itself except an extreme need continually desiring, and an extreme desire continually needing. And therefore, its whole life can be nothing else except a plague and torment of covetousness, envy, pride, and wrath, all of which are precisely nature, self, or hell.

The first three elements of nature: covetousness, pride, and envy, are not three different things, but only three different names for the restless workings of the same will or desire as it differently torments itself. There is nothing in any of them except the working of a restless desire, and this is because the natural life of the creature can do nothing else but operate as a desire. Therefore, when a created being has fallen from God, its first three consequences, which are quite inseparable from it, are covetousness, envy, and pride. It must covet because covetousness is a desire proceeding from lack. It must envy because envy is a desire turned to self. It must assume control because such lack of control is a desire founded on a real want for exaltation or a higher state.

Now wrath, which is the fourth element of self, nature, and hell, can have no existence until some or all of the first three are contradicted or have something done to them that is contrary to their will. Then wrath is necessarily born, and not until then. These four properties generate one another, and therefore generate their own torment. They have no outward cause, or any inward power of altering themselves. And therefore, all self or human nature must be in this state until some supernatural good comes into it. Therefore, every pain or disorder in the mind or body of any intelligent creature is an undeniable proof that it is in a fallen state and has lost that supernatural good for which it was created.

The fallen state of all mankind is a certain truth. Here lies the absolute, indispensable necessity of the one Christian redemption. Until fallen man is born again from above, until such a supernatural birth is brought forth in him by the eternal Word and Spirit of God, he can have no possible escape or deliverance from these four elements of self and hell.

While man lives among the vanities of time, his covetousness, envy, pride, and wrath may be in a tolerable state and may help him to have a mixture of peace and trouble. Men may have at times their gratifications, as well as their torments. But when death has put an end to the vanity of all earthly deception, the soul that is not born again of the supernatural Word and Spirit of God must find itself unavoidably devoured or shut up in its own, insatiable, unchangeable, self-tormenting covetousness, envy, pride, and wrath.

The serpents of covetousness, envy, pride, and wrath are alone the real, dreadful, original serpents; and all earthly serpents are but transitory, partial, and weak outbirths of them. All evil, earthly beasts are merely short-lived images or created, natural eruptions of that hellish disorder that is broken out from the fallen spiritual world. By their manifold variety, they show us the multiplicity of evil that lies in the womb of the abyss of dark rage that has no maker except the three first properties of nature fallen from God and working in their darkness.

The life of all evil, mischievous, ravenous, venomous beasts begins in and from this material world and totally ends at the death of their bodies. They have no malignity in their earthly, temporary natures except from the same wrathful properties of fallen nature that live and work in our eternal, fallen souls. Therefore, though they are as different from us as time is from eternity, wherever we see them, we see so many infallible proofs of the fall of nature and the reality of hell. If hell had not broken out in spiritual nature, not only no evil beast but also no bestial life could ever have come into existence.

I hope I have sufficiently opened unto you the malignant nature of self that dwells in and makes up the working life of every creature that has lost its right state in God. I hope that I have shown that all the evil that was in the first chaos of darkness or that is still in hell and devils—all the evil that is in material nature and material creatures, whether animate or inanimate—is nothing else and operates solely by those first properties of nature that drive on the life of fallen man in covetousness, envy, pride, and wrath.

Therefore, it is absolutely necessary to know that the nature and power of divine love is perfect peace and joy, a freedom from all disquiet, making everything to rejoice in itself. It is the Christ of God, and wherever it comes, it comes as the blessing and happiness of every natural life; as the restorer of every lost perfection; a redeemer from all evil; a fulfiller of all righteousness; and a *"peace of God, which passeth all understanding"* (Phil. 4:7). This knowledge should lead us to be a thousand times more than ever athirst after the spirit of love. We should be willing to sell all and buy it. Its blessing is so great and the lack of it so dreadful a state that we should even be afraid of lying down in our beds until every working power of our souls is given up to it, wholly possessed and governed by it.

Chapter 10

The Absolute
Importance of Faith

After going over all that there is to know about the spirit of love, you may be asking what it means to be saved from the mouth of Satan, the depth of all subtlety, the one who deceives the whole world. He can hide himself under all forms of goodness; he can pray and fast, write and instruct, pray much and preach long, give alms to the poor, visit the sick, and yet he often gets more life and strength and a more permanent place of residence through these forms of virtue than he has through more obvious forms of sin.

The solution to this contradiction is that there is no need for a number of external practices or methods in this matter. To die to self or to come from under its power cannot be done by any active resistance that we can make to it by the powers of nature. This is because nature can no more overcome or suppress itself than wrath can heal wrath. As long as nature acts, nothing but natural works are brought forth; therefore, the more labor of this kind, the more nature is fed and strengthened with its own food.

But the one true way of dying to self is most simple and plain. It needs no plans or methods, no cells, monasteries, or pilgrimages. It is equally practicable by everybody, and it is always at hand. It meets you in everything. It is free from all deceit and is never without success. If you ask what this one true, simple, plain, immediate, and unerring way is, it is the way of patience, meekness, humility, and yieldedness to God. This is the truth and perfection of dying to self. It is nowhere else, and it is not possible for it to be in anything else except in this state of heart.

DELIVERANCE FROM SELF

Most people readily acknowledge the excellency and perfection of these virtues, but many wonder as to how these virtues will prove that the way of overcoming self is so simple, plain, immediate, and unerring. This is because the doctrine of almost all men and all books, and confirmed by our own woeful experience, is that a great length of time and effort and a variety of practices and methods are necessary and scarcely sufficient in order to attain any one of these four virtues.

The solution to this problem is that when Christ our Savior was upon earth, there was nothing more simple, plain, immediate, or unerring than the way to Him. Did scribes, Pharisees, publicans, and sinners need any length of time or any exercise of rules and methods before they could have admission to

Him, or have the benefit of faith in Him? Such a question not only relates to, but is also the very heart and truth of, the matter before us. It is not a mere illustration of our subject, but is our subject itself, only set in a truer and stronger light.

When I refer you to patience, meekness, humility, and yieldedness to God as the one simple, plain, immediate, and unerring way of dying to self or being saved from it, it is because you can have all the benefit of these virtues as easily and immediately, without plan or method, as the publicans and sinners could turn to Christ and be saved. You have only to turn your faith to Christ, and you will die to self and be saved from it.

I say again: if you turn and give yourself up to these virtues, you will as certainly and immediately be directly possessed and blessed by their good power as when sinners turned to Christ to be helped and saved by Him. You may believe that this is too short a way and has too much of a miracle in it to be expected now, but I want you strictly to believe all this in the fullest sense of the words. And you should also believe that the reasons why you or anyone else is vainly endeavoring for a long time after and hardly ever attaining these first-rate virtues is that you seek them in the way they are not to be found. You seek them in the multiplicity of human rules, methods, and contrivances, and not in that simplicity of faith in which those who applied to Christ immediately obtained what they asked of Him.

"Come unto me, all ye that labour and are heavy laden, and I will give you rest" (Matt. 11:28). How short and simple and certain a way to peace and comfort from the misery and burden of sin! What

will now become of your length of time and effort, your rules and methods and roundabout ways to be delivered from self, the power of sin, and to find the redeeming power and virtue of Christ? Will you say that turning to Christ in faith was once indeed the way for Jews and heathens to enter into life and be delivered from the power of their sins, but that all this happiness ended as soon as Pontius Pilate nailed the good Redeemer to the cross? Could that have broken off all immediate union and communion between faith and Christ?

It would be foolish to suppose that Christ, after having finished His great work, overcome death, and ascended into heaven with all power in heaven and on earth, had become less of a Savior and gave less certain and immediate helps to those who by faith turn to Him now than when He was clothed with the infirmity of our flesh and blood upon earth. Does He have less power after He has conquered than while He was only resisting and fighting our enemies? Or does He have less goodwill to assist His church, His own body, now that He is in heaven than He had to assist publicans, sinners, and heathens before He was glorified as the Redeemer of the world? Yet this must be the case if our simply turning to Him in faith and hope is not as sure a way of obtaining immediate assistance from Him now as it was when He was upon earth.

You may then ask, Will turning in faith and desire toward patience, meekness, humility, and yieldedness to God do as fully for me now all that faith in Christ did for those who became His disciples? My reply to such a question is the following: Let it be supposed that I had given you a form of prayer in

94

these words: "O Lamb of God, who takes away the sins of the world, O Bread who came down from heaven, and You who are the resurrection and the life, the light and peace of all holy souls, help me to a living faith in You." Would you say that this was not a prayer of faith in and to Christ because it did not call Him Jesus or the Son of God? I would hope that you would answer that this is a true and good prayer to Jesus, the Son of the living God. For who else was the Lamb of God and the Bread who came down from heaven?

WHAT FAITH MEANS

When I exhort you to give yourself up, in faith and hope, to patience, meekness, humility, and yieldedness to God, what else do I do but turn you directly to so much faith and hope in the true Lamb of God? If I ask you what the Lamb of God is and means, you must tell me that it is and means the perfection of patience, meekness, humility, and yieldedness to God. Can you say it is either more or less than this? You must therefore say that a faith of hunger, thirst, and desire for these virtues is, in spirit and truth, the very same thing as a faith of hunger, thirst, and desire for salvation through the Lamb of God.

Consequently, you must also say that every sincere wish and desire, every inward inclination of your heart that presses after these virtues and longs to be governed by them, is an immediate, direct application to Christ, is worshipping and falling down before Him, is giving up yourself unto Him and the very perfection of faith in Him.

If you distrust my words, hear the words of Christ Himself: *"Learn of me; for I am meek and lowly in heart: and ye shall find rest unto your souls"* (Matt. 11:29). Here you have the plain truth fully asserted of what it means to give yourselves up in faith. First of all, to be given up to, or to strongly desire patience, meekness, humility, and yieldedness to God is strictly the same thing as to learn of Christ or to have faith in Him. Secondly, the one simple, short, and infallible way to overcome or be delivered from all the malignity and burden of self is expressed in the words, *"and ye shall find rest unto your souls."*

This simple tendency or inward inclination of your heart to sink down into patience, meekness, humility, and yieldedness to God is truly giving up all that you are and all that you have from fallen Adam. It is perfectly leaving all that you have to follow and be with Christ; it is your highest act of faith in Him and love for Him, the most ardent and earnest declaration of your cleaving to Him with all your heart and seeking no salvation except in Him and from Him. Therefore, all the good and blessing, pardon, and deliverance from sin that ever happened to anyone from any degree of faith, hope, and application to Christ is sure to come from this state of heart that continually turns to Him in a hunger and desire for being led and governed by His spirit of patience, meekness, humility, and yieldedness to God.

If only I could help you to perceive or feel what a good there is in this state of heart, you would desire it with more eagerness than the thirsty deer desires the water brooks (Ps. 42:1). You would think of nothing, desire nothing but to live in it constantly. It is a security from all evil and all delusion. There is no difficulty or trial either of body or mind, no temptation either within you or outside of you except what has its full remedy in this state of heart. You have no questions to ask of anybody, no new way that you need to inquire after, no oracle that you need to consult, for while you shut yourself up in patience, meekness, humility, and yieldedness to God, you are in the very arms of Christ. Your whole heart is His dwelling place, and He lives and works in you as certainly as He lived and governed that body and soul that He took from his mother, Mary.

CHRIST IS FOUND IN THE VIRTUES OF HIS CHARACTER

Learn whatever else you will from men and books, or even from Christ Himself, without these virtues, and you are only a poor wanderer in a barren wilderness where no water of life is to be found. Christ is nowhere but in these virtues, and wherever they are is His own kingdom. From morning to night, let this be the Christ whom you follow, and then you will fully escape all the religious delusions that are in the world and, what is more, all the delusions of your own selfish heart.

To seek to be saved by patience, meekness, humility, and yieldedness to God is truly coming to God through Christ. When these heavenly inclinations live and abide in you as the spirit and aim of your life, then Christ is truly in you, and the life that you then lead is not yours but Christ's, who lives in you (Gal. 2:20). This is following Christ with all your power. You cannot possibly move toward Him any more quickly. You have no other way of walking as

He walked, no other way of being like Him, of truly believing in Him, of showing your trust in Him and dependence upon Him, except by wholly giving yourself up to what He was, that is, to patience, meekness, humility, and yieldedness to God.

THE TOTAL DESPAIR OF SELF

I hope that I have so far proved to you the short, simple, and certain way of destroying that body of self that lives and works in the four elements of covetousness, envy, pride, and wrath. If covetousness had no power over you, you could have no other selfish inclinations to struggle against. They are all dead as soon as covetousness has finished working in you. Its nature is as large as desire, and wherever selfish desire is, there is all the evil nature of covetousness.

Now envy, pride, hatred, or wrath can have no possibility of existence in you unless there is some selfish desire alive in you that is not satisfied, not gratified, but resisted and disappointed. Therefore, as long as any selfish inclinations, whether of envy, uneasiness, complaint, pride, or wrath, are alive in you, you have the fullest proof that all these inclinations are born and bred in your own covetousness, that is, from that same selfish, bad desire that is called covetousness when it is turned to the wealth of this world.

All these four elements of self or fallen nature are tied together in one inseparable band. They are mutually generated from one another, they have only one common life, and they must all live or all die together. This may show you again the absolute necessity of our one simple and certain way of dying to self and the absolute insufficiency of all human means to bring this about.

Consider only this: to be angry at our own anger, to be ashamed of our own pride and strongly resolve not to be weak, is the outcome of all human endeavors, and yet all this is the life rather than the death of self. There is no help unless there is a total despair of all human help. When a man is brought to such an inward, full conviction as to have no more hope from all human means than he has hope to see with his hands or hear with his feet, then he is truly prepared to die to self. In other words, he is ready to give up all thoughts of having or doing anything that is good in any other way but that of a meek, humble, patient, total yielding up of himself to God.

Everything that we do before we come to this conviction is in great ignorance of ourselves and is full of weakness and impurity. Our zeal may be ever so wonderful, yet if it begins sooner or proceeds further to any other matter or in any other way than as it is led and guided by this conviction, it is full of delusion. No repentance, however long or laborious, is a true conversion to God until it falls into this state. God must do all, or all is nothing; but God cannot do all, until all is expected from Him. And all is not expected from Him until we have no hope, trust, or longing after anything but a patient, meek, humble, total yieldedness to God by a true and good despair of every human help.

Chapter 11

True Yieldedness
to God

Now, I have brought you to the very place where I desired this discussion to go: to set your feet upon sure ground with regard to the spirit of love. All the different subjects we have passed through have only been a variety of proofs that the spirit of divine love can have no place or possibility of existing in any fallen man until he desires and chooses to be dead to all self in a patient, meek, humble resignation to the good power and mercy of God.

From this state of heart, the spirit of prayer is also born, which is the desire of the soul that has turned to God. Stand, therefore, steadfastly in this will, and let nothing else enter into your mind. Do not have any other contrivance except to nourish and keep up this state of heart everywhere and in everything. Then your house is built upon a rock. You are safe from all danger. The light of heaven and the love of God will begin their work in you and will bless and sanctify every power of your fallen soul. You will be ready for every kind of virtue and good work and will know what it is to be led by the Spirit of God.

APART FROM FEELING

You may now be concerned that you should find yourself so overcome with your own darkness and selfish inclinations that you are not able to sink from them into an awareness of this meek, humble, patient, full resignation to God. You may then ask, What must I do, or how will I have the benefit of what you have taught me? If so, you are then at the very time and place of receiving the fullest benefit from it and practicing it with the greatest advantage to yourself.

For though this patient, meek resignation is to be exercised with regard to all outward things and occurrences of life, it chiefly deals with our own inward state: the troubles, perplexities, weaknesses, and disorders of our own fallen souls. To stand turned to a patient, meek, humble resignation to God when your own impatience, wrath, pride, and unyieldedness attacks you, is a higher and more beneficial performance of this duty than when you stand turned to meekness and patience when attacked by the pride or wrath or disorderly passions of other people.

I tell you, stand turned toward this patient, humble resignation, for this is your true performance of this duty at that time. Though you may have no comforting awareness of your performing it, in this state you may always have one full proof of the truth and reality of it, that is, when you seek for help in no other way, and in nothing else, neither from men nor books, but wholly give yourself up to be helped by the mercy of God. And thus, whatever your state may be, you may always have the full benefit of this short and sure way of yielding yourself up to God. The greater the perplexity of your distress is, the nearer you are to the greatest and best relief, provided that you have patience to expect it all from God. Nothing brings you so near to divine relief as the extremity of distress.

The goodness of God is nothing other than Him being the Helper of all who want to be helped. Nothing can possibly hinder you from finding this goodness of God and every other gift and grace that you stand in need of. Nothing can hinder or delay it unless you turn from the only fountain of life and living water to some cracked cistern of your own making. You can also hinder or delay it by turning to some method, opinion, division, or subdivision among Christians who are carnally expecting some mighty things either from Samaria or Jerusalem, Paul or Apollos. These things are only and solely to be had by worshipping the Father in spirit and in truth, and this is only done when your whole heart, soul, and spirit trust wholly and solely in the operation of God within you, in whom *we live, and move, and have our being* (Acts 17:28).

Be assured of this as a most certain truth: we have neither more nor less of the divine operation within us because of any particular outward form or manner of our lives. We only have it in the degree to which our faith, hope, trust, and dependence upon God are more or less in us.

It is foolish, then, to be so often perplexed about the way to God. Nothing can be the way to God except our hearts. God is to be found nowhere else, and the heart itself cannot find Him or be helped by anything else to find Him but by its own love for Him, faith in Him, dependence upon Him, yieldedness to Him, and expectation of all from Him.

These are short but full points of true faith that carry salvation along with them, that make a true and full offering of our whole natures to the divine operation, and also a true and full confession of the Holy Trinity in unity. As they look wholly to the Father as blessing us with the operation of His own Word and Spirit, so they truly confess and worship the Holy Trinity of God. And as they ascribe all to and expect all from this Deity alone, they make the truest and best of all confessions: there is no God but one. Your foundation stands sure while you look for all your salvation through the Father, who works life in your soul by His own Word and Spirit that dwell in Him and are one life, both in Him and you.

TOTAL RESIGNATION

I hope that now you can always know how to find full relief in this humble, meek, patient, total resignation of yourself to God. It is, as I have said, a remedy that is always at hand, equally practicable at all times, and never in greater reality than when your own inclinations are making war against it in your own heart.

The God of patience, meekness, and love is the one God of my heart, and yours, too, I hope. The whole bent and desire of your soul should be to seek all your salvation in the merits and mediation of the meek, humble, patient, yielded, suffering Lamb of God who alone has power to bring forth these heavenly virtues in your soul. He is the Bread of God who came down from heaven, of which the soul must eat, or else it will perish and pine in everlasting hunger. He is the eternal love and meekness who left the bosom of His Father, to be Himself the resurrection of meekness and love in all the darkened, wrathful souls of fallen men.

What a comfort is it to think that this Lamb of God, the Son of the Father, the Light of the World, who is the glory of heaven and the joy of angels, is as near to us and as truly in the midst of us as He is in the midst of heaven. And there is not a thought, look, or desire of our hearts that presses toward Him, longing to catch one small spark of His heavenly nature, that is not as sure a way of finding Him, touching Him, and drawing virtue from Him as the woman who was healed by longing only to touch the border of His garment. (See Matthew 9:20–22.)

This doctrine should make you weary and ashamed of all your own natural inclinations. Every whisper of your soul that stirs up impatience, uneasiness, resentment, pride, and wrath within you should be rejected with a *"Get thee behind me, Satan"* (Luke 4:8), for it is his and has its whole nature from him. It is quite a frightful thing to rejoice in a resentment that has been gratified. In reality, it is but rejoicing that my own serpent of self has new life and strength given to it, and that the precious Lamb of God is denied entrance into my soul.

This is the strict truth of the matter. To give in to resentment and to gratify it willingly is calling up the courage of your own serpent and truly helping it to be more stout and valiant and successful in you. On the other hand, to give up all resentment of every kind and on every occasion, however skillfully, beautifully, and outwardly colored such resentment may be, and to sink down into the humility of meekness under all conflict, contradiction, and injustice, always turning the other cheek to the smiter (Matt. 5:39), however haughty, is the best of all prayers. This is the surest of all means to have nothing but Christ living and working in you as the Lamb of God who takes away every sin that ever had power over your soul. (See John 1:29.)

Oh, sweet resignation of myself to God, happy death of every selfish desire, blessed unction of a holy life, the only driver of all evil out of my soul, be my guide and governor wherever I go! Nothing but this can take me from myself; nothing but this can lead me to God. Hell has no power where such resignation is, and heaven cannot hide itself from it. Oh, may I never indulge a thought, bring forth a word, or do anything for myself or others but under the influence of this blessed aspiration.

THE ABSOLUTE NECESSITY OF THE DEATH OF SELF

If you ever go aside from the path of meekness, humiliation, and patience, even if the occasion may seem ever so glorious, or the effects ever so wonderful to you, it is only preparing for yourself a harder death. For you must die to everything that you have done under any other spirit except that of meekness, humility, and true yieldedness to God. Everything else, no matter what it is, has its life from the fire of

106

nature. It belongs to nothing else and must be given up, lost, and taken from you again by fire, either here or hereafter. These virtues of meekness, humiliation, and patience are the only wedding garment; they are the lamps and vessels well furnished with oil. (See Matthew 25:1–13.)

There is nothing that can take the place of the virtues I have talked about. They must have their own full and perfect work in you, if not before, then certainly after the death of the body, or else the soul can never be delivered from its fallen, wrathful state. And all this is no more than is implied in the Scripture doctrine that says there is no possibility of salvation except by an indwelling of the meek, humble, patient, fully yielded Lamb of God in our souls. And when this Lamb of God has brought forth a real birth of His own meekness, humility, and full resignation to God in our souls, then our lamps are trimmed and our virgin hearts are made ready for the marriage feast.

The marriage feast signifies the entrance into the highest state of union that can be between God and the soul in this life. Or, in other words, it is the birthday of the spirit of love in our souls. When this happens, the spirit of love will fill our souls with such peace and joy in God as will blot out the remembrance of everything that we once called peace or joy.

As surely as the light of God is absolutely necessary to make nature a heavenly kingdom of light and love, so must created life that is fallen from God under the wrathful first properties of nature surely have no deliverance from it. Created life cannot have a birth of heavenly light and love by any other possible way but that of dying to self by meekness, humility, patience, and full resignation to God.

The reason for all this is that the will is the leader of created life, and a creature can have nothing but what its will is turned to. Therefore, it cannot be saved from or raised out of the wrath of nature until its will turns from nature and determines to be no longer driven by it. But it cannot turn from nature or show a desire to come from under its power in any other way than by turning and giving itself up to that meekness, humility, patience, and resignation to God. This turning and giving up is a leaving, rejecting, and dying to all the guidance of nature.

THE ONE INFALLIBLE WAY TO GOD

Thus you see that this one simple way is, according to the immutable nature of things, the only possible and absolutely necessary way to God. It is as possible to go two contrary ways at once as it is to go to God any other way than this. But what is best of all is that this way is absolutely infallible. Nothing can defeat it. And all this infallibility is fully grounded in the twofold character of our Savior: as He is the Lamb of God, a principle and source of all meekness and humility in the soul, and as He is the Light of eternity who blesses eternal nature and turns it into a kingdom of heaven.

For in this twofold respect, He has the power to redeem us, which nothing can hinder. But sooner or later, He must see all His and our enemies under His feet, and all that is fallen in Adam into death must rise and return to a unity of eternal life in God.

For as the Lamb of God, He has all power to bring forth in us an awareness and a weariness of our own wrathful state and a willingness to fall from it into meekness, humility, patience, and resignation to the mercy of God, which alone can help us. When we are weary and heavy laden and willing to give rest to our souls in meek, humble, patient resignation to God, then He, as the light of God and heaven, joyfully breaks in upon us, turns our darkness into light and our sorrow into joy, and begins that kingdom of God and divine love within us that will never have an end.

Need I say more to show you how to come out of the wrath of your evil, earthly nature into the sweet peace and joy of the spirit of love? Neither ideas, nor speculations, nor devotion, nor fervor, nor rules, nor methods can bring it forth. It is the child of light and cannot possibly have any birth in you except solely from the light of God rising in your own soul, just as it rises in heavenly beings. But the light of God cannot arise or be found in you by any method or contrivance of your own, except through the meekness, humility, and patience that waits, trusts, yields to, and expects all from the inward, living, life-giving operation of the triune God within you, creating, quickening, and reviving in your fallen soul that birth and image and likeness of the Holy Trinity in which the first father of mankind was created.

By a variety of points, I hope that I have fixed and confirmed you in a full belief of that great truth, namely that there is but one salvation for all mankind, and that is the life of God in the soul. And also I hope I have proven to you that there is but one possible way for man to attain this life of God, not one for a Jew, another for a Christian, and a third for a heathen. No, God is one, human nature is one, salvation is one, and the way to it is one. This one thing is the desire of the soul turned to God.

Part II

The Spirit of Eternity

Chapter 12

The Entrance of Evil into the World

Most people may be said to be asleep, and this is even more true of Christians. The particular way of life that takes up each man's mind, thoughts, and actions may be very well called his particular dream. This degree of vanity is equally visible in every form and order of life. The educated and the uneducated, the rich and the poor, are all in the same state of slumber, only passing away a short life in different kinds of dreams. But why is this so?

It is because man has an eternity within him. He is born into this world, not for the sake of living here, not for anything this world can give him, but only to have time and place to become either an eternal partaker of a divine life with God or to have an hellish eternity among fallen angels. Therefore, every man whose eye, heart, and hands are not continually governed by this twofold eternity, may justly be said to be fast asleep and to have no awakened awareness of himself.

THE VANITY OF TIME

A life devoted to the interests and enjoyments of this world, spent and wasted in the slavery of earthly desires, may be truly called a dream, since such a life has all the shortness, vanity, and delusion of a dream. There is one great difference, though, between a dream and this life: when a dream is over, nothing is lost but fictions and fancies, but when the dream of life is ended only by death, all that eternity for which we were brought into being is lost.

Now there is no misery in this world, nothing that makes either the life or death of man to be full of calamity, except this blindness and unawareness of man's state, into which he so willingly, and even obstinately, plunges himself. Everything that has the nature of evil and distress in it arises from here. Suppose that a man knows himself, that he comes into this world on no other errand except to rise out of the vanity of time into the riches of eternity; suppose that he governs his inward thoughts and outward actions by this view of himself; then every day to him has lost all its evil. Prosperity and adversity have no difference, because he receives and uses them both in the same spirit. Life and death are equally welcome, because they are equal parts of his way to eternity.

THE ONLY GOOD

As poor and miserable as this life is, we have free access to all that is great and good, and we carry within ourselves a key to all the treasures that heaven has to bestow upon us. We might starve in the midst of plenty and groan under infirmities, but the remedy is in our own hands.

Some of us live and die without ever knowing and feeling anything of the only good, while we have it in our power to know and enjoy it in as great a reality as we know and feel the power of this world over us. Heaven is as near to our souls as this world is to our bodies, and we are created and redeemed to have our conversation in it (Phil. 3:20). God, the only good of all intelligent natures, is not an absent or distant God, but is more present in and to our souls than our own bodies are. We are strangers to heaven, and we are without God in the world, because we are void of the spirit of prayer that alone can, and never fails to, unite us with the only good and that can open heaven and the kingdom of God within us.

A root set in the finest soil, grown in the best climate, and blessed with all that sun and air and rain can do for it, is not as sure to grow to perfection as every man may be whose spirit aspires after all that God is ready to give to him. For the sun does not meet the springing bud that stretches toward him with half the certainty that God, the source of all good, Himself communicates to the soul that longs to partake of Him.

MAN CREATED IN THE IMAGE OF GOD

All of us are the offspring of God by birth, more nearly related to Him than we are to one another, *"for in him we live, and move, and have our being"*

(Acts 17:28). The first man who was brought forth from God had the breath and spirit of the Father, Son, and Holy Spirit breathed into him, and so he became a living soul (Gen. 2:7). This is how our first father was born of God, descended from Him, and stood in Paradise in the image and likeness of God. He was the image and likeness of God, not with regard to his outward shape or form, for no shape has any likeness to God; but he was in the image and likeness of God because the Holy Trinity had breathed their own nature and spirit into him. And as the Deity, Father, Son, and Holy Spirit, is always in heaven and makes heaven to be everywhere, so this spirit, breathed into man, brought heaven into man along with it. So, man was in heaven, as well as on earth, that is, in Paradise, which signifies a heavenly state of life.

MAN IN PARADISE

Adam had the same divine nature, both as a heavenly spirit and a heavenly body, that the angels have. But as he was brought forth to be a lord and ruler of a new world, created out of the chaos or ruins of the kingdom of fallen angels, it was necessary that he should also have the nature of this new created world in himself, both its spirit and materiality. This is why he had a body taken from this newly created earth, the same dead earth from which we now make bricks. He was taken from the blessed earth of Paradise that had the powers of heaven in it, out of which the Tree of Life itself could grow.

Into the lungs of this outward body, the breath or spirit of this world was breathed. In the spirit and body of this world, the inward celestial spirit and body of Adam did dwell. It was the medium or means through which he was to have commerce with this world, become visible to its creatures, and rule over it and them. This is where our first father stood: an angel both as to body and spirit—as he will be again after the resurrection—yet dwelling in a body and spirit taken from this new, created world. This world, however, was as inferior to him and as subject to him as the earth and all its creatures were. It was no more alive in him; it no more brought forth its nature within him than Satan and the Serpent were alive in him at his first creation. He was to have no share of its life and nature, no feeling of good or evil from it, but he was to act in it as a heavenly artist who had power and skill to open the wonders of God in every power of outward nature.

And in this lay the ground of Adam's ignorance of good and evil. It was because his outward body and the outward world—in which alone was good and evil—could not discover their own natures or open their own lives within him, but were kept inactive by the power and life of the celestial man within him. This was man's first great trial. It was a trial not imposed upon him by the mere will of God or by way of experiment, but a trial necessarily implied by the nature of his state.

Man was created as an angel, both in body and in spirit, and this angel stood in an outward body that had the nature of the outward world. Therefore, by the nature of his state, he had his trial, or power to choose, whether he would live as an angel, using only his outward body as a means of opening the wonders of the outward world to the glory of his creator, or whether he would turn his desire to the opening of the bestial life of the outward world in himself for the sake of knowing the good and evil that was in it. The fact is certain that he lusted after the knowledge of this good and evil and made use of the means to obtain it. As soon as he had gotten this knowledge by opening the bestial life within him, his soul, an immortal fire that could not die, became a poor slave in the prison of bestial flesh and blood.

THE NATURE OF REDEMPTION

The nature and necessity of our redemption is to redeem the first angelic nature that departed from Adam. It is to make that heavenly spirit and body that Adam lost become alive again in all human nature, and this is called regeneration. This is the true reason why only the Son, or eternal Word of God, could be our Redeemer. It is because He alone, by whom all things were made at first, is able to bring to life again the celestial spirit and body that had departed from Adam.

The need for us to regain our first heavenly body is the same as the need for us to eat the body and blood of Christ. The need for again having our first heavenly spirit is declared by the need for our being baptized by the Holy Spirit. Our fall is nothing else except the falling of our souls from this celestial body and spirit into a bestial body and spirit of this world. Our rising out of our fallen state, or redemption, is nothing else except the regaining of our first angelic spirit and body, which in Scripture is called our inward or new man, created again in Christ Jesus.

Lastly, this is the true reason why the mortification of flesh and blood is required in the Gospel. It is because the bestial life of this outward world should never have been opened in man. The natural life is his separation from God and death to the kingdom of heaven; therefore, all its workings, appetites, and desires are to be restrained and kept under so that the first heavenly life, to which Adam died, may have room to rise in us.

It is plain that the command of God not to lust after and eat of the forbidden tree was not an arbitrary command of God given for His pleasure or as a mere trial of man's obedience. But it was kind and loving information given by the God of love to His newborn offspring concerning the state he was in and concerning the outward world. It warned him to withdraw all desire of entering into an awareness of the tree's good and evil, because such sensibility could not be had without his immediately dying to that divine and heavenly life that he then enjoyed. The God of love said, *"Of the tree of the knowledge of good and evil, thou shalt not eat of it: for in the day that thou eatest thereof thou shalt surely die"* (Gen. 2:17).

THE FALL OF THE ANGELS AND THE CREATION OF THE WORLD

To better understand all this, imagine if God had said the following to the newly created Adam. "I have brought you into this Paradise, with such a nature as the angels have in heaven. By the order and dignity of your creation, everything that lives and moves in this world is made subject to you. I have made you in your outward body of this world to be for a time a little lower than the angels until you have brought forth numerous offspring fit for that kingdom that they have lost.

"The world around you, and the life that is newly awakened in it, is much lower than you are. It is of a nature quite inferior to yours. It is a gross, corruptible state of things that cannot stand long before Me but must for a while bear the marks of those creatures, which first made evil to be known in the creation.

"The angels, who first inhabited this region where you are to bring forth a new order of beings, were great and powerful spirits, highly endowed with the riches and powers of their Creator. While they stood, as the order of creation requires, in meekness and resignation under their Creator, nothing was impossible to them; there was no end of their glorious powers throughout their whole kingdom. Perpetual scenes of light, glory, and beauty were rising and changing through all the height and depth of their glassy sea, merely at their will and pleasure.

"But they began to admire and even adore themselves because of the wonders of light and glory that they could perpetually bring forth. They discovered how all the powers of eternity, treasured up in their glassy sea, unfolded themselves and broke forth in ravishing forms of wonder and delight, merely in obedience to their call. They began to imagine that there was some infinity of power hidden in themselves that they supposed was kept under and suppressed by that meekness and subjection to God under which they acted.

"Fired and intoxicated with this proud idea, they boldly resolved, with all their eternal energy and strength, to take their kingdom to themselves, with all its glories, by eternally renouncing all meekness and submission to God. No sooner did their eternal, potent desires fly in the direction of a revolt from God, than in the swiftness of a thought, heaven was lost, and they found themselves to be dark spirits, stripped of all their light and glory. Instead of rising above God, as they had hoped, by breaking off from Him, there was no end of their eternal sinking into new depths of slavery under their own self-tormenting natures.

"Just as a wheel that is going down a mountain that has no bottom must continually keep turning, so these angels are whirled down by the impetuosity of their own wrongly turned wills, in a continual descent from the fountain of all glory into the bottomless depths of their own dark, fiery powers. They are in no hell except what their own natural strength had awakened. They are bound in no chains except their own unbending, hardened spirits. They have been made such by their renouncing, with all their eternal strength, all meekness and subjection to God. In that moment, the beautiful materiality of their kingdom, their glassy sea in which they dwelt, was broken into pieces by the wrathful, rebellious workings of these apostate spirits, and it became a black lake, a horrible chaos of fire and wrath, thickness and darkness, a height and depth of the confused, divided, struggling properties of nature.

"My creating decree stopped the workings of these rebellious spirits by dividing the ruins of their wasted kingdom into an earth, a sun, stars, and other elements. If this revolt of angels had not brought forth that disordered chaos, the materiality of the outward world would never have been known. The raw, compacted earth, stones, rocks, wrathful fire here, dead water there, contending elements, with all their coarse vegetables and animals, are things not known in eternity and will only be seen in time until the great designs are finished, for which you are brought forth in Paradise. And then, just as a fire awakened by the rebel creature began all the disorders of nature and turned that glassy sea into a chaos, so a last fire, kindled at My word, will thoroughly purge the floor of this world. In those purifying flames, the sun, the stars, the air, the earth, and the water will part with all their dross, deadness, and division. They will then all become again that first, heavenly materiality, a glassy sea of everlasting light and glory, in which you and your offspring will sing hallelujahs for all eternity.

"Therefore, child of Paradise, son of eternity, do not look with a longing eye after anything in this outward world. There are the remains of the fallen angels in it; you have nothing to do in it except be a ruler over it. It stands before you as a mystery big with wonders, and you, while an angel in Paradise, have power to open and display them all. It does not stand in your sphere of existence. It is only a picture and a transitory image of things, for all that is not eternal is only like an image in a mirror that seems to have a reality, which it does not have.

"The life that springs up in this image of a world, in such an infinite variety of kinds and degrees, is only like a shadow; it is a life of such days and years that in eternity have no distinction from a moment. It is a life of such animals and insects that are without any divine sense, capacity, or feeling.

Their natures have nothing in them except what I commanded this new modeled chaos, this order of stars and fighting elements, to bring forth.

"In heaven, all births and growths, all figures and spiritual forms of life, though infinite in variety, are yet all of a heavenly kind and are only so many manifestations of the goodness, wisdom, beauty, and riches of the divine nature. But in this newly modeled chaos, where the disorders that were raised by Lucifer are not wholly removed, every kind and degree of life, like the world from which it springs, is a mixture of good and evil in its birth. And both evil and good must stand here in strife until the last purifying fire.

"Therefore, my son, be content with your angelic nature. Be content, as an angel in Paradise, to eat angels' food and to rule over this mixed, imperfect, and perishing world without partaking of its corruptible, impure, and perishing nature. Do not lust to know how the animals feel the evil and good that this life affords them, for if you could feel what they feel, you must be as they are. You cannot have their awareness unless you have their nature. You cannot be an angel and an earthly animal at the same time. If the bestial life is raised up in you, the heavenly birth of your nature must die in you at the same instant.

"Therefore, turn away your lust and your mind from a tree that can only help you to the knowledge of such good and evil that belongs only to the animals of this outward world, for nothing but the bestial nature can receive good or evil from the stars and elements. They have no power over anything except over that life that proceeds from them.

Therefore, eat only the food of Paradise, and be content with angels' bread.

"And if you eat of this tree, it will unavoidably awaken and open the bestial life within you, and in that moment, all that is heavenly must die and cease to have any power in you. Then, you will fall into a slavery for life, under the divided struggling powers of stars and elements. Stripped of any angelic garment that hid your outward body under its glory, you will become more naked than any beast upon earth and will be forced to seek a covering from beasts, to hide you from the sight of your own eyes. You will be a shameful, fearful, sickly, needy, suffering, and distressed heir of the same speedy death in the dust of the earth as the poor beasts, whom you will thus have made to be your brothers."

Chapter 13

The Need for
a New Birth

God, considered in Himself, is as infinitely separate from all possibility of doing harm, or wanting pain to come to any creature, as He is from a possibility of suffering pain or hurt from the hand of a man. And this is so for the plain reason that He is in Himself, in His Holy Trinity, nothing else but the boundless depths of all that is good and sweet and amiable. Therefore, He stands in the utmost opposition to everything that is not a blessing, in an eternal impossibility of intending a moment's pain or hurt to any creature. For, from this unbounded source of goodness and perfection, nothing but infinite streams of blessing are perpetually flowing forth upon all nature and all creatures in a more incessant plenty than rays of light stream from the sun.

As the sun has only one nature and can give forth nothing but the blessings of light, so the holy triune God has only one nature and intent toward all creation, which is to pour forth the riches and sweetness of His divine perfections upon everything that is capable of receiving them and according to its capacity to receive them.

LOVE IS THE NATURE OF GOD

The goodness of God breaking forth into a desire to communicate good was the cause and the beginning of the creation. Therefore, for all eternity, God can have no thought or intent toward His creation except to communicate good, because He made the creature for the sole end to receive good. The first motive toward the creature is unchangeable. It arises from God's desire to communicate good, and it is an eternal impossibility that anything can ever come from God, as His will and purpose toward His creation, except that same love and goodness that first created it. God must always desire for His creation what He desired at the creation of it.

This is the amiable nature of God: He is the good, the unchangeable, overflowing fountain of good, who sends forth nothing but good for all eternity. He is the love itself, the unmixed, unmeasurable love, doing nothing except what comes from love, giving nothing except gifts of love to everything that He has made. And He requires nothing of all His creatures except the spirit and fruits of that love that brought them into being.

Oh, how sweet is this contemplation of the height and depth of the riches of divine love! With what attraction must it draw every thoughtful man to return love for love to this overflowing fountain of boundless goodness! What charms does that religion have that makes us aware of our existence in, relation to, and dependence upon this ocean of divine love! Look closely at every part of our redemption, from Adam's first sin to the resurrection of the dead, and you will find nothing but successive mysteries of that first love that created angels and men. All the mysteries of the Gospel are only many marks and proofs of God's desiring to make His love triumph in the removal of sin and disorder from all nature and creation.

CHRIST DELIVERS US

But let us return and further consider the nature of Adam's fall. See here the deep basis and absolute necessity of that new birth of the Word, Son, and Spirit of God that the Scriptures speak so much of. It is because our souls, now that we are fallen, are quite dead to and separate from the kingdom of heaven by having lost the light and Spirit of God. Therefore, our souls are necessarily incapable of entering into heaven, until by this new birth the soul gets again its first heavenly nature.

If you have nothing of this birth when your body dies, then you have only the root of life in you that the devils have. You are as far from heaven and as incapable of it as they are; your nature is their nature, and therefore their habitation must be yours. For nothing can possibly hinder your union with fallen angels when you die except a birth in your soul of what the fallen angels have lost.

The doctrine that the fallen soul is in this real state of death is not only plain from the whole tenor of Scripture, but is also affirmed in all systems of divinity. For every Bible scholar holds and teaches that unredeemed man, at the death of his body, will have fallen into a state of misery like that of the fallen angels. But how can this be true, unless it is also true that the life of heaven was extinguished in the soul and that man had really lost the light and Spirit of God that alone can make anyone capable of living in heaven? Therefore, all that I have said here and elsewhere concerning the death of the soul by its fall, and its needing a real new birth of the Son and Holy Spirit of God in it in order to receive salvation, cannot be denied except by giving up this great, fundamental doctrine: that unredeemed man in his fallen state must have been eternally lost. It cannot be true that the fall of unredeemed man would have kept him forever out of heaven unless his fall had absolutely put an end to the life of heaven in his soul.

On the other hand, it cannot be true that Jesus Christ is his Redeemer and delivers him from his fallen state unless it is true that Jesus Christ helps him to a new birth of that light and Spirit of God that was extinguished by his fall. Nothing could possibly be the redemption or recovery of man except regeneration alone. His misery was his having lost the life and light of heaven from his soul, and therefore nothing in all the universe of nature except a new birth of what he had lost could be his deliverance from his fallen state.

Therefore, if angels after angels had come down from heaven to assure him that God had no anger for him, he would still have been in the same helpless state. And if they had told him that God had pity and compassion toward him, he would have been even more hindered, because nothing could make even a beginning of his deliverance except

what made a beginning of a new birth in him.
Nothing could fully bring about his recovery except
what perfectly finished the new birth of all the
heavenly life that he had lost.

PARTAKERS OF THE DIVINE NATURE

One might wonder how any persons who believe
the great mystery of our redemption, who adore the
depths of the divine goodness—in that the Son of
God, the second person in the Trinity, became a man
Himself in order to make it possible for man to enter
again into the kingdom of God—should yet seek and
contend for not a real, but a figurative sense of a
new birth in Jesus Christ. Is there anything more
inconsistent than this? Or can anything strike more
directly at the heart of the whole nature of our redemption? God became man, and He took upon
Himself a birth from the fallen nature. But why was
this done? Or in what does the adorable depth of this
mystery lie? How does all this manifest the infinity
of the divine love toward man?

It is because nothing less than this mysterious
incarnation, which astonishes even the angels, could
open a way, or begin a possibility, for fallen man to
be born again from above and made again a partaker
of the divine nature. It was because man had become
so dead to the kingdom of heaven that there was no
help for him through all nature. No powers, no abilities of the highest order of creatures, could kindle
the least spark of life in him or help him to the least
glimpse of that heavenly light that he had lost.

All nature and created beings stood around
Adam and were unable to help him, as he was unable

to help himself, because what he had lost was the life and light of heaven. How glorious the mystery is that enables us to say that when man was made incapable of any relief from all the powers and possibilities of nature, then the Son, the Word of God, entered by a birth into this fallen nature. And by this mysterious incarnation, all of fallen nature might be born again through Him according to the Spirit, in the same reality as fallen nature was born of Adam according to the flesh. Look at this mystery in this true light, in this plain sense of Scripture, and then you must be forced to fall down before it in adoration of it. For all that is glorious and good with regard to man is manifestly contained in it.

This new birth is not a part, but the whole of our salvation. Everything in religion, from the beginning to the end of time, is only for the sake of the new birth. Nothing does us any good unless it either helps forward our regeneration or is a true fruit or effect of it. All the glad tidings of the Gospel, all the benefits of our Savior, however variously expressed in Scripture, all center in the following: that He has become our Light, our Life, our Resurrection, our Holiness, and our Salvation; and that we are new creatures in Him, created again into righteousness, born again of Him, of the Spirit of God from above. Everything in the Gospel is for the sake of this new creature, this new man in Christ Jesus, and nothing is taken into consideration without it.

UNION WITH CHRIST

"I am the vine, ye are the branches" (John 15:5). Here Christ, our Second Adam, uses this metaphor

to teach us that the new birth we are to have from Him is real in the strictest and most literal sense of the words. He also is teaching us that there is the same close relationship between Him and His true disciples that there is between the vine and its branches. He does in us and for us all that the vine does for its branches. Now the life of the vine must really be derived into the branches; they cannot be branches until the life of the vine is brought forth in them. Therefore, as surely as the life of the vine must be brought forth in the branches, we must be born again through our Second Adam. Unless the life of the holy Jesus is in us through a birth from Him, we are as dead to Him and the kingdom of God as the branch is dead to the vine from which it is broken off.

Again our blessed Savior says, *"Without me ye can do nothing"* (v. 5). The question is, When, or how, may a man be said to be without Christ? Consider again the vine and its branches: a branch can only be said to be without its vine when the vegetable life of the vine is no longer in it. This is the only sense in which a man can be said to be without Christ. When He is no longer in us, as a principle of a heavenly life, we are then without Him and can do nothing, that is, nothing that is good or holy.

A Christ not in us is the same thing as a Christ not ours. If all we have of Christ is to own and receive the history of His birth, person, and character, we are as much without Him, as much left to ourselves, as little helped by Him, as those evil spirits who cried out, "[We] *know thee who thou art, the Holy One of God"* (Mark 1:24). Those evil spirits, and all the fallen angels, are totally without Christ and have no benefit from Him, for this one and only reason, because Christ is not in them. Nothing of the Son of God is generated or born in them. Therefore, every son of Adam who does not have something of the Son of God generated or born within him is as much without Christ, as destitute of all help from Him, as those evil spirits who could only make an outward confession of Him.

CHRIST WITHIN US

It is the language of Scripture that Christ in us is our hope of glory (Col. 1:27). Christ formed in us, living, growing, and raising His own life and spirit in us, is our only salvation. And indeed, all this is plain from the nature of creation and man. Since the Serpent, sin, death, and hell are all essentially within us and are the very essence of our nature, must not our redemption be equally inward, an inward essential death to this state of our souls, and an inward growth of a contrary life within us?

If Adam were only an outward person, if his whole nature were not our nature, born in us and derived from him into us, it would be nonsense to say that his fall is our fall. In the same way, if Christ, our Second Adam, were only an outward person; if He did not enter as deeply into our nature as the first Adam does; if we do not have from Him a new inward, spiritual man as truly as we have outward flesh and blood from Adam; what ground could there be to say that our righteousness is from Him as our sin is from Adam?

There should be no room here for anyone to charge me with disregard to the holy Jesus, who was born of the Virgin Mary, or with setting up an inward Savior in opposition to the outward Christ, whose history is recorded in the Gospel. No, it is with the utmost fullness of faith and assurance that I ascribe all our redemption to that blessed and mysterious Person, who was then born of the Virgin Mary. I will assert no inward redemption except what wholly proceeds from, and is brought about by, that life-giving Redeemer, who died on the cross for our redemption.

If I were to say that a plant or vegetable must have the sun within it, must have the life, light, and virtues of the sun incorporated in it, that it has no benefit from the sun until the sun is thus inwardly forming, generating, quickening, and raising up a life of the sun's virtues in it, would this be setting up an inward sun in opposition to the outward one? Could anything be more ridiculous than such an accusation? The same that is here said of an inward sun in the vegetable is said of a power and virtue derived from the sun in the heavens. In the same way, all that is said of an inward Christ, inwardly formed, and generated in the root of the soul, is only what is said of an inward life, brought forth by the power and efficacy of that blessed Christ, who was born of the Virgin Mary.

Chapter 14

The Life of Christ in Us

You have seen, dear reader, the nature and necessity of regeneration. Therefore, be fully persuaded to believe, and to settle firmly in your mind this most certain truth, that all our salvation consists in the manifestation of the nature, life, and spirit of Jesus Christ in our inward new man. This alone is Christian redemption; this alone delivers us from the guilt and power of sin; this alone redeems, renews, and regains the first life of God in the soul of man.

Everything besides this is self, falsehood, propriety, your own will, and, however colored, it is only your old man with all his deeds. Enter into this truth, therefore, with all your heart. Let your eyes always be upon it. Do everything in view of it. Try everything by the truth of it. Love nothing except for the sake of it. Wherever you go, whatever you do, at home or abroad, in the field or at church, do everything out of a desire for union with Christ, in imitation of His tempers and inclinations, and look upon everything as nothing, except for what exercises and increases the spirit and life of Christ in your soul. Keep Jesus in your heart from morning to night; long for nothing, desire nothing, hope for nothing, except to have all this within you changed into the spirit and temper of the holy Jesus. Let this be your Christianity, your church, and your religion.

THE WAY TO THE NEW BIRTH

This new birth in Christ, thus firmly believed and continually desired, will do everything that you want to have done in you. It will dry up all the springs of vice and stop all the workings of evil in your nature; it will bring all that is good into you. It will open all the Gospel within you, and you will know what it is to be taught of God. This longing desire of your heart to be one with Christ will soon put a stop to all the vanity of your life, and nothing will be allowed to enter into your heart, or proceed from it, except what comes from God and returns to God. You will soon be tied and bound in the chains of all holy inclinations and desires; your mouth will be kept from saying unholy things; your ears will willingly hear nothing that does not draw you to God; and your eyes will not be open to anything except to see and find occasions of doing good.

When this faith has reached both your head and your heart, it will then be with you as it was with the merchant who found a pearl of great price (see Matthew 13:45–46); it will make you gladly sell all that you have in order to buy it. Everything that has seized and possessed your heart, whether riches, power, honor, education, or reputation, will lose all its value and will be easily parted with as soon as this glorious pearl, the new birth in Christ Jesus, is discovered and found by you.

But perhaps you will say, How will this great work, the birth of Christ, be brought about in me? Instead it might be said, since Christ has an infinite power and also an infinite desire to save mankind, How can anyone miss out on this salvation except through his own unwillingness to be saved by Him? How was it that the lame and blind, the lunatic and leper, the publican and sinner, found Christ to be their Savior and to do for them all that they wanted to be done for them? It was because they had a real desire of having what they asked for, and therefore in true faith and prayer, they applied to Christ that His Spirit and power might enter into them and heal what they wanted and desired to be healed in them.

They all said in faith and desire, *"Lord, if thou wilt, thou canst make me* [whole]" (Matt. 8:2). And the answer was always this, *"As thou hast believed, so be it done unto thee"* (Matt. 8:13). This is Christ's answer now, and thus it is done to every one of us at this day; as our faith is, so is it done unto us. And here lies the whole reason of our falling short of the salvation of Christ: it is because we have no desire for it.

WHAT THE SALVATION OF CHRIST CONSISTS OF

But you will say, Do not all Christians desire to have Christ as their Savior? Yes, but here is the deceit: all want Christ to be their Savior in the next world, and to help them into heaven when they die, by His power and merits with God. But this is not desiring Christ to be your Savior; for His salvation, if it is had, must be had in this world. If He saves you, it must be done in this life by changing and altering all that is within you, by helping you to a new heart, as He helped the blind to see, the lame to walk, and the dumb to speak.

To have salvation from Christ is nothing else but to be made like Him. It is to have His humility and meekness; His mortification and self-denial; His renunciation of the spirit, wisdom, and honors of this world; His love for God; and His desire to do God's will and to seek only His honor. To have these qualities formed and begotten in your heart is to have salvation from Christ. But if you do not want to have these tempers brought forth in you, if your faith and desire do not seek and cry to Christ for them in the same way as the lame asked to walk and the blind asked to see, then you must be said to be unwilling to have Christ as your Savior.

Again, consider, how was it that the carnal Jew, the well-read scribe, the learned rabbi, the religious Pharisee, not only did not receive, but also crucified their Savior? It was because they did not want and desire the Savior that He was. They did not want the inward salvation that He offered to them. They did not desire any change of their own natures, any inward destruction of their own natural tempers, any deliverance from the love of themselves and the enjoyments of their passions.

These Jews liked their carnal states, the gratifications of the old man, their long robes, their large ornaments, and their greetings in the markets. They

did not want to have their pride and self-love de-
throned, their covetousness and sensuality subdued
by a new nature from heaven derived into them.
Their only desire was the success of Judaism; they
wanted to have an outward savior, a temporal
prince, who would establish their laws and ceremonies over all the earth. And therefore, they crucified
their dear Redeemer and would have none of His
salvation, because it all consisted in a change of their
natures, in a new birth from above, and a kingdom
of heaven to be opened within them by the Spirit of
God.

Oh, Christians, do not look only at the Jews of
old, but see yourselves in this light. May the sad
truth be told that on this day, a Christ within us, an
inward Savior raising a birth of His own nature, life,
and spirit within us, is rejected as foolishness or fanaticism. The learned rabbis take offense at it. The
propagation of Catholicism, the propagation of Prot-
estantism, the success of some particular church, is
the salvation about which priests and people are
chiefly concerned.

HOW THE BIRTH OF CHRIST IS TO BE BROUGHT ABOUT IN US

It is evident that the only way by which one
cannot get the benefit of Christ's salvation is
through an unwillingness to have it, and from the
same spirit and tempers that made the Jews unwilling to receive it. But if you want to know further
how this great work, the birth of Christ, is to be
brought about in you, then let this joyful truth be
told to you, that this great work is already begun in
every one of us.

This holy Jesus, who is to be formed in you, who is to be the Savior and new life of your soul, who is to raise you out of the darkness of death into the light of life and give you power to become a son of God, is already within you, living, stirring, calling, knocking at the door of your heart, and wanting nothing but your own faith and good will. Jesus wants to have as real a birth and form in you as He had in the Virgin Mary.

The eternal Word, or Son of God, did not first begin to be the Savior of the world when He was born in Bethlehem of Judea. The Word that became man in the Virgin Mary did, from the beginning of the world, enter as a Word of Life, a Seed of Salvation, into the first father of mankind. He was inspoken into him, as an ingrafted Word, under the name and character of a Bruiser of the Serpent's head. This is why Christ said to His disciples, *"The kingdom of God is within you"* (Luke 17:21); that is, the divine nature is within you, given unto your first father, into the light of his life, and from him it has risen in the life of every son of Adam.

This is also why the holy Jesus is said to be the *"Light, which lighteth every man that cometh into the world"* (John 1:9). He was not said to be the Light of every man who comes into the world because He was born at Bethlehem and He had a human form upon earth. But He is called so because He is that eternal Word, by which all things were created, which was the life and light of all things, and which had entered again into fallen man as a Second Creator, as a Bruiser of the Serpent. In this respect, it was truly said of our Lord, when on earth, that He was that *"Light, which lighteth every man that cometh into the world."* He was really and truly all this, as He was the Immanuel, the God with us, given unto Adam and to all his offspring through him.

When our blessed Lord conversed with the woman at Jacob's well, He said to her, *"If thou knewest the gift of God, and who it is that* [speaks] *to thee...thou wouldest have asked of him, and he would have given thee living water"* (John 4:10). Anyone may well say that this woman of Samaria was very happy to stand so near this gift of God, from whom she might have had living water, if she would only have asked for it. But, dear Christian, this happiness is yours, for this holy Jesus, the Gift of God, first given to Adam, and in him to all who are descended from him, is the gift of God to you, as sure as you are born of Adam. Even more, if you have never yet owned Him, if you have wandered from Him as far as the Prodigal Son from his father's house, He is still with you. He is the Gift of God to you, and if you will turn to Him and ask of Him, He has living water for you.

FINDING CHRIST THROUGH TURNING TO THE HEART

Poor sinner, consider the treasure you have within you: the Savior of the world. The eternal Word of God lies hidden in you as a spark of the divine nature that is to overcome sin and death and hell within you, and to generate the life of heaven again in your soul. Turn to your heart, and your heart will find its Savior, its God within itself. You see, hear, and feel nothing of God because you seek Him abroad with your outward eyes. You seek Him in books, in controversies, in the church, and in outward exercises, but you will not find Him there until you have first found Him in your heart. Seek Him in your heart, and you will never seek in vain, for He dwells there and the seat of His light and Holy Spirit is there.

This turning to the light of God within you is your only true turning to God. There is no other way of finding Him except in that place where He dwells in you. For though God is present, He is only present to you in the deepest and most central part of your soul. Your natural senses cannot possess God or unite you to Him. Even more, your inward faculties of understanding, will, and memory can only reach after God, but they cannot be the place of His habitation in you. But there is a root or depth in you, from which all these faculties come forth as lines from a center, or as branches from the body of a tree. This depth is called the center, the fund, or the bottom of the soul. This depth is the unity, the eternity—I had almost said, the infinity—of your soul, for it is so infinite that nothing can satisfy it or give it any rest, except the infinity of God.

In this depth of the soul, the Holy Trinity brought forth its own living image in the first created man, bearing in himself a living representation of the Father, Son, and Holy Spirit, and this was his dwelling in God and God in him. This was the kingdom of God within him and made into Paradise outside of him. But the day that Adam ate of the forbidden earthly tree, in that day he absolutely died to this kingdom of God within him. This depth or center of his soul, having lost its God, was shut up in death and darkness, and it became a prisoner in an earthly animal that only excelled its fellow created beings, the beasts, in an upright form and serpentine subtlety. Thus ended the fall of man.

But from the moment that the God of mercy spoke the Bruiser of the Serpent into Adam, from that moment all the riches and treasures of the divine nature again came into man, as a seed of salvation sown into the center of the soul. It only lies hidden there in every man, until he desires to rise from his fallen state and to be born again from above.

Chapter 15

The Pearl
of Eternity

To continue my discussion on what it means to give up all for Christ, I will now show a little more distinctly what the pearl of eternity is. You should begin to search and dig into your own field for the pearl of eternity that lies hidden in it. It cannot cost you too much, and you cannot buy it for too much, for it is everything. When you have found it, you will know that all you have sold or given away for it is like nothing, like a bubble upon the water.

THE LIGHT AND SPIRIT OF GOD WITHIN YOU

Up until now, this light and Spirit within you have done you little good, because all the desire of your heart has been after the light and spirit of this world. Your reason and senses, your heart and passions, have turned all their attention to the poor

145

concerns of this life, and therefore you are a stranger to this principle of heaven, these riches of eternity within you. For as God is not and cannot truly be found by any worshippers, except those who worship Him in spirit and in truth, so this light and Spirit, though always within us, are not and cannot be found, felt, or enjoyed, except by those whose whole spirit is turned to them.

When man first came into being and stood before God as His own image and likeness, this light and Spirit of God were as natural to him, were as truly the light of his nature, as the light and air of this world are natural to the creatures that have their birth in it. But when man, not content with the food of eternity, ate of the earthly tree, this light and Spirit of heaven then became no more natural to him, and they no more rose up as a birth of his nature. Instead, he was left solely to the light and spirit of this world. And this is that death, which God told Adam he would surely die in the day that he would eat of the forbidden tree.

But the goodness of God would not leave man in this condition. A redemption from it was immediately granted, and the Bruiser of the Serpent brought the light and Spirit of heaven once more into the human nature. It was not brought in as it was in its first state, when man was in Paradise. It was brought in as a treasure hidden in the center of our souls, which should reveal and open itself by degrees in the proportion that the faith and desires of our hearts are turned to it.

This light and Spirit of God thus freely restored again to the soul, and lying in it as a secret source of heaven, are called grace, free grace, or the supernatural gift or power of God in the soul. They are called this because they were something that the natural powers of the soul could no more obtain. This is why, in the greatest truth and highest reality, every stirring of the soul, every tendency of the heart toward God and goodness, is justly and necessarily ascribed to the Holy Spirit or the grace of God.

This first seed of life, which is sown into the soul as the gift or grace of God to fallen man, is itself the light and Spirit of God. Therefore, every stirring or opening of this seed of life, every awakened thought or desire that arises from it, must be called the moving or the quickening of the Spirit of God. Then the new man who arises from it must be said to be solely the work and operation of God.

In this we also have a clear declaration of the true meaning and certain truth of all those Scriptures that speak of the inspiration of God, the operation of the Holy Spirit, and the power of the divine light as the sole and necessary agents in the renewal and sanctification of our souls, and also as being things common to all men. It is because this Seed of Life, or Bruiser of the Serpent, is common to all men and has in all men a degree of life, which is in itself so much of the inspiration, or life, Spirit, and light of God. And this is in every soul, and it is the soul's power of becoming born again of God.

Therefore, all men are exhorted not to quench or resist or grieve the Spirit, that is, this seed of the Spirit and light of God that is in all men as the only source of good. Again, *"the flesh lusteth against the Spirit, and the Spirit against the flesh"* (Gal. 5:17). Mere human nature, or the natural man as he is by the Fall, is what is meant by the flesh and its lustings.

The Bruiser of the Serpent, that Seed of the light and Spirit of God that lies as a treasure hidden in the soul in order to bring forth the life that was lost in Adam, is what is meant by the spirit. Now, just as the flesh has its life and its lustings from which all sorts of evil are truly said to be inspired, quickened, and stirred up in us, so the spirit, being a living principle within us, has its inspiration, its breathing, its moving, and its quickening from which alone the divine life, or the angel that died in Adam, can be born in us.

See here, in short, the redeemed state of man. He has a spark of the light and Spirit of God, as a supernatural gift of God given into the birth of his soul, to bring forth by degrees a new birth of the life that was lost in Paradise. This holy spark of the divine nature within him has a natural, strong, and almost infinite tendency toward that eternal light and Spirit of God from which it came forth. It came forth from God; it came out of God; it partook of the divine nature; and therefore it is always in a state of tendency toward returning to God. And all this is called the breathing, the moving, and the quickening of the Holy Spirit within us, which are the operations of this spark of life that tends toward God.

On the other hand, the Deity, as considered in itself and without the soul of man, has an infinite, unchangeable tendency of love and desire toward the soul of man. The Deity wants to unite and communicate its own riches and glories to man's soul, just as the spirit of the air outside of man, unites and communicates its riches and virtues to the spirit of the air that is within man. This love or desire of God toward the soul of man is so great that He gave His only begotten Son, the brightness of His glory, to take upon Him the human nature in its fallen state. He did this so that by this mysterious union of God and man, all the enemies of the soul of man might be overcome, and every human creature might have the power of being born again according to that image of God in which he was first created.

The Gospel is the history of this love of God for man. Inwardly, he has a seed of the divine life in the birth of his soul, a seed that has all the riches of eternity in it and is always wanting to be born in him and be alive in God. Outwardly, he has Jesus Christ, who as a Sun of Righteousness is always casting forth His enlivening beams on this inward seed, to kindle and call it forth to the birth. Jesus does to the seed of heaven in man what the sun in the firmament is always doing to the vegetable seeds in the earth.

Consider this matter in the following metaphor. A grain of wheat has the air and light of this world enclosed or incorporated in it. This is the mystery of its life. This is its power of growing. By this it has a strong continual tendency of uniting again with that ocean of light and air, from which it came forth, and so it helps to kindle its own vegetable life. On the other hand, that great ocean of light and air, having its own offspring hidden in the heart of the grain, has a perpetual strong tendency to unite and communicate with it again. From this desire for union on both sides, the vegetable life arises, and all the virtues and powers are contained in it.

But let it be well observed here that this desire on both sides cannot have its effect until the husk and bulk of the grain fall into a state of decay and death. Until this begins, the mystery of life hidden in it cannot come forth. We may see here the true basis for and absolute necessity of that dying to ourselves, and to the world, to which our blessed Lord so constantly calls all His followers. A universal self-denial, a perpetual mortification of the lust of the flesh, the lust of the eyes, and the pride of life, is not a thing imposed upon us by the mere will of God. It is not required as a punishment, is not an invention of dull and monkish spirits, but it is as absolutely needed to make way for the new birth as the death of the husk and bulk of the grain is necessary to make way for the vegetable life.

THE WISDOM AND LOVE OF GOD WITHIN YOU

In this pearl of eternity, all the holy nature, spirit, tempers, and inclinations of Christ lie as a seed in the center of your soul. Divine wisdom and heavenly love will grow up in you, if you give only true attention to God who is present in your soul. On the other hand, there is hidden also in the depth of your nature the root or possibility of all the hellish nature, spirit, and inclinations of the fallen angels. For both heaven and hell have their foundations within us. They do not come into us from outside, but they spring up in us, according to our wills and hearts, depending if they are turned either to the light of God or to the kingdom of darkness. But when this life, which is in the midst of these two eternities, is at an end, either an angel or a devil will be found to have a birth in us.

Therefore, you do not need to run here or there, saying, Where is Christ? You do not need to say,

The Pearl of Eternity

Who shall ascend into heaven? (that is, to bring Christ down from above:) or, Who shall descend into the deep? (that is, to bring up Christ again from the dead.) (Rom. 10:6–7)

Behold, the Word, which is the wisdom of God, is in your heart. It is there as a Bruiser of the Serpent, as a Light unto your feet and a Lantern unto your paths (Ps. 119:105). It is there as a holy oil to soften and overcome the wrathful fiery properties of your nature and to change them into the humble meekness of light and love. It is there as a speaking word of God in your soul. As soon as you are ready to hear, this eternal speaking word will speak wisdom and love in your inward parts and bring forth the birth of Christ, with all His holy nature, spirit, and inclinations, within you.

This is why there has been in all ages in the Christian church, even among the most illiterate, both men and women who have attained a deep understanding of the mysteries of the wisdom and love of God in Christ Jesus. And it is no wonder, since it is not an art or a science, or a skill in grammar or logic, but the opening of divine life in the soul that can give true understanding of the things of God. This life of God in the soul, which is compared to a grain of mustard seed by our Lord (Matt. 13:31) because of its smallness at first and capacity for great growth, may be, and generally is, suppressed and kept under, either by worldly cares or pleasures, or by vain learning, sensuality, or ambition.

On the other hand, wherever this seed of heaven is allowed to take root, to get life and breath in the soul, whether it is in man or woman, young or old, there this newly born inward man is justly said to be inspired, enlightened, and moved by the Spirit of God. This is because his whole birth and life is a birth from above, of the light and Spirit of God; therefore, all that is in him has the nature, spirit, and tempers of heaven in it. As this regenerate life grows up in any man, a true and real knowledge of the whole mystery of godliness in himself grows up.

All that the Gospel teaches about sin and grace, about life and death, about heaven and hell, about the new and old man, about the light and Spirit of God, are things not gotten by hearsay, but inwardly known, felt, and experienced in the growth of his own newborn life. He then has an anointing from above that teaches him all things. He has a Spirit that knows what it ought to pray for (Rom. 8:26), a Spirit that prays without ceasing (1 Thess. 5:17), a Spirit that is risen with Christ from the dead (Rom. 8:11) and has all its conversation in heaven (Phil. 3:20), a Spirit that has groans and sighs that cannot be uttered (Rom. 8:26), a Spirit that travails and groans with the whole creation (v. 22) to be delivered from vanity and have its glorious liberty in that God from whom it came forth.

THE TEMPLE OF GOD WITHIN YOU

This pearl of eternity is the consecrated place of divine worship, where alone you can worship God in spirit and in truth. You can worship Him in spirit because your spirit is the one thing in you that can unite and cleave unto God and receive the workings of His divine Spirit upon you. This is because this adoration in spirit is the truth and reality of which all outward forms and rites, though instituted by God, are only representative now of the true worship that is to come. However, the worship itself is eternal.

Accustom yourself to the holy service of this inward temple. In the midst of it is the fountain of living water, of which you may drink and live forever. There the mysteries of your redemption are celebrated, or rather opened in life and power. There the supper of the Lamb is kept; the Bread that came down from heaven, which gives life to the world, is your true nourishment. All of this is done, and known in real experience, in a living awareness of the work of God in the soul. There the birth, the life, the sufferings, the death, the resurrection, and the ascension of Christ are not merely remembered, but they are also inwardly found and enjoyed as the real state of your soul, which has followed Christ in the regeneration.

Once you are well grounded in this inward worship, you will have learned to live unto God above time and place. For every day will be Sunday to you, and wherever you go, you will have a priest, a church, and an altar along with you. When God has all that He should have of your heart, then everything you do will be a song of praise, and the common business of your life will be a conforming to God's will on earth, as angels do in heaven. Then you will renounce the will, judgment, tempers, and inclinations of your old man. You will be wholly given up to the obedience of the light and Spirit of God within you, to will only His will, to love only in His love, to be wise only in His wisdom.

THE PEACE AND JOY OF GOD WITHIN YOU

Finally, this pearl of eternity can only be found by the manifestation of the life and power of Jesus Christ in your soul. But Christ cannot be your power and your life until, in obedience to His call, you deny yourself, take up your daily cross, and follow Him in the regeneration. (See Matthew 16:24.) This is peremptory; it allows for no reservations or evasion; it is the one way to Christ and eternal life. But, wherever you are, either here or in Rome or Geneva, if self is not denied, if you live for your own will, for the pleasures of your natural lust and appetites, senses and passions, and in conformity to the vain customs and spirit of this world, you are dead while you live. Christ can profit you nothing. You are a stranger to all that is holy and heavenly within you, and you are utterly incapable of finding the peace and joy of God in your soul.

Therefore, you will be poor and blind and naked and empty and will live a miserable life in the vanity of time, while all the riches of eternity, the light and Spirit, the wisdom and love, the peace and joy of God are within you. And thus it will always be with you. There is no remedy; go wherever you will, do whatever you will, all is shut up. There is no door of salvation, no awakening out of the sleep of sin, no deliverance from the power of your corrupt nature, no overcoming of the world, no revelation of Jesus Christ, no joy of the new birth from above, until, dying to yourself and the world, you turn to the light, Spirit, and power of God in your soul. All is fruitless and insignificant; all the means of your redemption are at a standstill; all outward forms are but a dead formality, until this fountain of living water is found within you.

HOW TO POSSESS THIS PEARL OF ETERNITY

But you will perhaps say, "How will I discover these riches of eternity, this light and Spirit and wisdom and peace of God, treasured up within me?" Your first thought of repentance, or desire of turning to God, is your first discovery of this light and Spirit of God within you. It is the voice and language of the Word of God within you, though you do not know it. It is the Bruiser of the Serpent's head, your dear Immanuel, who is beginning to preach within you the same thing He first preached in public, saying, *"Repent ye: for the kingdom of heaven is at hand"* (Matt. 3:2).

When, therefore, the smallest instinct or desire of your heart calls you toward God and a newness of life, give it time and permission to speak. Take care that you do not refuse Him who speaks. For it is not an angel from heaven who speaks to you, but it is the eternal speaking Word of God in your heart. That Word which at first created you is thus beginning to create you a second time unto righteousness so that a new man may be formed again in you in the image and likeness of God.

But above all things, beware of taking this desire of repentance to be the effect of your own natural sense and reason, for in so doing you lose the key of all the heavenly treasure that is in you. You shut the door against God, turn away from Him, and your repentance—if you have any—will be only a vain, unprofitable work of your own hands that will do

155

you no more good than a well that has run dry. If you take this awakened desire of turning to God to be, as in truth it is, the coming of Christ in your soul, the working, redeeming power of the light and Spirit of the holy Jesus within you—if you reverence and adhere to it as such—this faith will save you and will make you whole. By believing so in Christ, though you were dead, yet you will live.

Now this all depends upon your right submission and obedience to this speaking of God in your soul. Therefore, stop all self-activity; do not listen to the suggestions of your own reason; do not run on in your own will; but be silent, passive, and humbly attentive to this newly risen light within you. Open your heart, your eyes, and your ears to all its impressions. Let it enlighten, teach, frighten, torment, judge, and condemn you as it pleases. Do not turn away from it; hear all that it says; seek no relief out of it; do not consult with flesh and blood, except with a heart full of faith and resignation to God. Only pray this prayer: that God's kingdom may come and His will be done in your soul. (See Matthew 6:10.) Stand faithfully in this state of preparation, thus given up to the Spirit of God, and then God will begin and carry out the work of your repentance. You will soon find that He who is in you is much greater than all who are against you (1 John 4:4).

DEPENDENCE ON GOD'S SPIRIT

So that you may better do all this and be more firmly assured that this yieldedness to and dependence upon the working of God's Spirit within you is right and sound, I will lay before you two great, infallible, and fundamental truths that will be as a rock for your faith to stand upon.

First, through the whole nature of things, nothing can be a real good to your soul except the operation of God upon it. Secondly, all the dispensations of God to mankind, from the fall of Adam to the preaching of the Gospel, were only for this one end: to fit, prepare, and order the soul for the operation of the Spirit of God upon it. Once these two great truths are well understood, the soul will be put in its right state: in a continual dependence upon God, and in a readiness to receive all good from Him. These truths will be a continual source of light in your mind. They will keep you safe from all error and false zeal in the things and forms of religion, from a sectarian spirit, from bigotry, and from superstition. They will teach you the true difference between the means and end of religion.

Chapter 16

The One Way
of Salvation

Man, by his fall, had broken off from his true center, his proper place in God. Therefore, the life and operation of God were not in him anymore. He had fallen from a life in God into a life of self, into an animal life of self-love, self-glorification, and self-seeking in the poor, perishing enjoyments of this world. This was the natural state of man due to the Fall. He was a defector from God, and his natural life was all idolatry, where self was the great idol that was worshipped instead of God. This is the whole truth in short. All sin, death, damnation, and hell are nothing else but this kingdom of self, or the various operations of self-love, self-glorification, and self-seeking, which separate the soul from God and end in eternal death and hell.

NATURE AND GRACE

On the other hand, all that is grace, redemption, salvation, sanctification, spiritual life, and the new birth is nothing else but the life and operation of God found again in the soul. It is man come back again into his center or place in God, from which he had broken off. The beginning again of the life of God in the soul was then first made when the mercy of God spoke a seed of the divine life into Adam, which would bruise the head of the Serpent that had worked itself into the human nature. Here the kingdom of God was again within us, though only as a seed; yet, small as it was, it was still a degree of the divine life that, if rightly cultivated, would overcome all the evil that was in us and make a newborn son of God of every fallen man.

THE OLD AND NEW TESTAMENT

All the sacrifices and institutions of the ancient patriarchs, the Law of Moses with all its types, rites, and ceremonies had this one end: they were the methods of divine wisdom for a time, in order to keep the hearts of men from the wanderings of idolatry in a state of holy expectation upon God. They were to keep the first seed of life in a state of growth and to make way for the further operation of God upon the soul, or, as the apostle said, to be as a schoolmaster unto Christ (Gal. 3:24). That is, they were to do so until the birth, the death, the resurrection, and the ascension of Christ should conquer death and hell, open a new dispensation of God, and baptize mankind afresh with the Holy Spirit and fire of heaven. Then, on the Day of Pentecost, a new dispensation of God came forth, which on God's part was the operation of the Holy Spirit in gifts and graces upon the whole church. On man's part, it was the adoration of God in spirit and in truth.

Thus, all that was done by God, from the Bruiser of the Serpent given to Adam, to Christ's sitting down on the right hand of God, was all for this end: to remove all that stood between God and man and to make way for the immediate and continual operation of God upon the soul. Then man, baptized with the Holy Spirit and born again from above, should absolutely renounce self and wholly give up his soul to the operation of God's Spirit. He should do so in order to know, to love, to will, to pray, to worship, to preach, to exhort, and to use all the faculties of his mind and all the outward things of this world as enlightened, inspired, moved, and guided by the Holy Spirit. By this last dispensation of God, this Spirit was given to be a Comforter, a Teacher, and a Guide to the church, to abide with it forever.

THE KINGDOM OF GOD

Christianity is a spiritual society, not because it has no worldly concerns, but because all its members are born of the Spirit, kept alive, animated, and governed by the Spirit of God. It is constantly called by our Lord the kingdom of God, or heaven, because all its ministry and service, all that is done in it, is done in obedience and subjection to that Spirit by which angels live and are governed in heaven. This is why our blessed Lord taught His disciples to pray that this kingdom might come so that God's will might be done on earth, as it is in heaven (Matt. 6:10). This could not happen, except by that same Spirit by which it is done in heaven.

The end result is this: the kingdom of self is the fall of man or the great apostasy from the life of God in the soul, and everyone, wherever he is, who lives for self is still under the Fall and great apostasy from God. The kingdom of Christ is the Spirit and power of God dwelling and manifesting itself in the birth of a new inward man, and no one is a member of this kingdom unless a true birth of the Spirit is brought forth in him. These two kingdoms comprise all of mankind. He who is not of one is certainly in the other; dying to one is living to the other.

SUBJECTION TO THE SPIRIT OF GOD

Here is shown the true basis and reason of what was said above, namely, that when the call of God to repentance first arises in your soul, you are to be silent, passive, and humbly attentive to this new risen light within you. You should do so by wholly stopping or disregarding the workings of your own will, reason, and judgment. It is because all these are false counselors, the sworn servants and bribed slaves of your fallen nature. They are all born and bred in your kingdom of self. Therefore, if a new kingdom is to be set up in you, if the operation of God is to have its effect in you, all these natural powers of self are to be silenced and suppressed until they have learned obedience and subjection to the Spirit of God.

Now this is not requiring you to become a fool, or to give up your claim to sense and reason, but it is the shortest way to have your sense and reason delivered from folly. It is the only way to have your whole rational nature strengthened, enlightened, and guided by that light, which is wisdom itself.

A child who obediently denies his own will and own reason to be guided by the will and reason of a truly wise and understanding tutor cannot be said to make himself a fool and give up the benefit of his rational nature. But rather, he is said to have taken the shortest way to have his own will and reason truly made a blessing to him.

THE NEED TO MORTIFY SELF

Why is it so necessary, then, that we universally mortify and deny ourselves with regard to all our senses, appetites, tempers, passions, and judgments? What is the basis for it? Our whole nature, which is fallen from the life of God, is in a state of discord with the order and end of our creation. It is a continual source of disorderly appetites, corrupt tempers, and false judgments. And therefore, every motion of it is to be mortified, changed, and purified from its natural state before we can enter into the kingdom of God.

Thus, when our Lord says, *"If any man come to me, and hate not his father, and mother, and wife, and children, and brethren, and sisters, yea, and his own life also, he cannot be my disciple"* (Luke 14:26), it is because our best inclinations are yet carnal and full of the imperfections of our fallen nature. This doctrine is just and good. It is not that father and mother are to be hated, but the love that an unregenerate person or natural man has toward them is to be hated. It should be hated because it is a blind self-love, full of all the weakness and partiality with which fallen man loves, honors, esteems, and cleaves to himself. This love, born from corrupt flesh and blood and polluted with self, is to be hated and parted with, so that we may love them with a love born of God—with such a love, and on such a motive, as Christ has loved us. And then the disciple of Christ, who loves with a love born of God, far exceeds all others in his love of parents, brother, sister, wife, and children.

And, our own lives are to be hated. The reason for this is plain: there is nothing lovely in them. They are a legion of evil, a monstrous birth of the Serpent, the world, and the flesh. They are an apostasy from the life and power of God in the soul, a life that is death to heaven, that is pure unmixed idolatry, that lives wholly to self and not to God. Therefore, all this self-life is to be absolutely hated, all this self is to be denied and mortified if the nature, spirit, tempers, and inclinations of Christ are to be brought to life in us. For it is as impossible to live both these lives at once, as for a person to move two opposite ways at the same time. Therefore, all these mortifications and self-denials have an absolute necessity in the nature of salvation itself.

FORSAKING ALL

Thus, when our Lord further says, Unless a man forsakes all that he has, he cannot be My disciple (Luke 14:33), the reason is plain and the necessity absolute. It is because all that the natural man has is in the possession of self-love, and therefore this possession is to be absolutely forsaken and parted with. All that he has is to be put into other hands, to be given to divine love, or else this natural man cannot be changed into a disciple of Christ. Self-love, in all that it has, is earthly, sensual, and devilish, and therefore must have all taken away from it. Then all is lost to the natural man. He has nothing left; all is laid at the feet of Jesus. And then all things are common (see Acts 2:44–45) as soon as self-love has lost the possession of them. Having nothing, yet possessing all things, all that the natural man has forsaken is restored a hundred times to the disciple of Christ.

Self-love, the greatest of all thieves, has now been cast out, and all that man had stolen and hidden has been taken from him and put into the hands of divine love. Therefore, every mite has become a large treasure, and material wealth opens the door into everlasting habitations. This was the Spirit of the first draft of a Christian church at Jerusalem: a church truly made after the pattern of heaven; where the love that reigns in heaven reigned in it; where divine love broke down all the selfish fences, the locks and bolts of me, mine, my own, and made all things common to all the members of this new kingdom of God on earth.

Now, though barely a few years passed after the age of the apostles before Satan and self got footing in the church and set up shop in the house of God, this one heart and Spirit, which first appeared in the Jerusalem church, is that same heart and Spirit of divine love to which all who would be true disciples of Christ are still called. Though the practice of it is lost as to the church in general, it ought not to have been lost.

Therefore, every Christian ought to make it his great care and prayer to have it restored in himself. And then, though born in the dregs of time, or living in Babylon, he will as truly be a member of the first heavenly church at Jerusalem as if he had lived in it in the days of the apostles. This Spirit of love, born of that celestial fire with which Christ baptizes His true disciples, is alone that Spirit that can enter into heaven. Therefore, it is that Spirit that is to be born in us while we are on earth. For no one can enter heaven until he is made heavenly, until the Spirit of heaven has entered into him. And therefore, all that our Lord has said of denying and dying to self, and of our parting with all that we have, are practices that are absolutely necessary.

THE LOVE OF OUR NEIGHBOR

Because all turning to self is turning from God, all that we have of a hellish, earthly weight must be taken off or there can be no ascension into heaven. But you will perhaps say, If all self-love is to be renounced, then all love of our neighbor is renounced along with it, because the commandment is only to love our neighbor as ourselves (Matt. 22:39). The answer here is easy, and yet there is no mention made of self-love. There is only one love in heaven, and yet the angels of God love one another in the same manner as they love themselves. The one supreme, unchangeable rule of love is a law to all intelligent beings of all worlds and will be a law for all eternity. It is that God alone is to be loved for Himself, and all other beings only loved through Him and for His sake. Whatever intelligent creature does not live under this rule of love is fallen from the order of his creation and is a defector from God and incapable of the kingdom of heaven until he returns to this eternal law of love.

Now if God alone is to be loved for Himself, then no creature is to be loved for itself, and so all self-love in every creature is absolutely condemned. And if all created beings are only to be loved through God and for His sake, then my neighbor is to be loved as I love myself, and I am only to love myself as I love my neighbor or any other created being for God's sake. And thus the command of loving our neighbor as ourselves stands firm, and yet all self-love is plucked up by the roots.

But what is loving any man only through God and for His sake? It is when we love him only because he is God's work, image, and delight; when we love him merely because he is God's and belongs to Him. This is loving him through God, and when all that we wish, intend, or do to him is done from a love of God, for the honor of God, and in conformity to the will of God, this is loving him for God's sake. This is the one love that is and must be the spirit of all creatures who live united to God.

Now this is no speculative refinement or finespun fantasy, but the simple truth and a first law of nature and a necessary kind of union between God and those He has created. The creature is not in God, is a stranger to Him, has lost the life of God in himself, whenever his love does not thus begin and end in God.

REDEEMED FROM SELF

The loss of this love was the fall of man, because it opened in him a kingdom of self in which Satan, the world, and the flesh could bring forth their own works. Therefore, if man is to rise from his fall and return to his life in God, there is an absolute necessity that self, with all its brood of corrupted inclinations, be deposed, that his first love for which he was created may be born again in him.

Christ came into the world to save sinners, to destroy the works of the Devil. Self is not only the seat and habitation of sin, but also the very life of it. The works of the Devil are all brought about in self; it is his special workhouse. Therefore, Christ does not come as a Savior from sin, as a Destroyer of the works of the Devil in any of us, except as far as self is beaten down and overcome in us.

If it is literally true what our Lord said, that His *"kingdom is not of this world"* (John 18:36), then it is a truth of the same certainty that no one is a member of this kingdom except he who in the literal sense of the words renounces the spirit of this world. Christians might as well part with half the articles of their creed, or only half believe them, if they even enter into these self-denials by halves. For all that is in the creed is only to bring forth this death to every part of the old man, so that the life and Spirit of Christ may be formed in us.

Our redemption is this new birth; if this is not done in us, we are still unredeemed. And though the Savior of the world is come, He is not come in us, He is not received by us, is a stranger to us, is not ours, if His life is not within us. His life cannot be within us, except as far as the spirit of the world, self-love, self-glorification, and self-seeking are renounced and driven out of us.

THE TRUE NATURE AND WORTH OF SELF-DENIAL

From all this we may also learn the true nature and worth of all self-denials and mortifications.

Their nature, considered in themselves, has nothing of goodness or holiness, and so they are not any real parts of our sanctification. They are not the true food or nourishment of divine life in our souls. They have no quickening, sanctifying power in them. Their only worth consists in this: that they remove the impediments of holiness, break down what stands between God and us, and make way for the quickening, sanctifying Spirit of God to operate on our souls. This operation of God is the only thing that can raise the divine life in the soul, or help it to the smallest degree of real holiness or spiritual life.

In our creation, we had only that degree of a divine life that the power of God derived into us. Since all that we had and were was the sole operation of God in the creation of us, in our redemption, or in regaining that first perfection that we have lost, all must again be the operation of God. Every degree of the divine life restored in us, no matter how small, must be nothing else except as much of the life and operation of God that is found again in the soul. All the activity of man in the works of self-denial has no good in itself but is only to open an entrance for the only good, the light of God, to operate upon us.

AVOID THE DANGER OF TRUSTING IN OUR SELF-DENIAL

We may also learn the reason why many people not only lose the benefit, but are even worse for all their mortifications. It is because they mistake the whole nature and worth of them. They practice them for their own sakes, as things good in themselves. They think them to be real parts of holiness, and so they rest in them and look no further, but grow full of self-glorification and self-admiration for their own progress in them. This makes them self-sufficient, morose, and severe judges of all those who fall short of their mortifications. And thus their self-denials do for them only what indulgences do for other people: they withstand and hinder the operation of God upon their souls, and instead of being real self-denials, they strengthen and keep up the kingdom of self.

There is no avoiding this fatal error except by deeply entering into this great truth: that all our own activity and effort has no good in it, can do no good for us, except as it leads and turns us in the best manner to the light and Spirit of God, which alone brings life and salvation into the soul. *"Stretch forth thine hand"* (Matt. 12:13), said our Lord to the man *"which had his hand withered"* (v. 10); he did so, and *"it was restored whole, like as the other"* (v. 13).

Now did this man have any basis for pride, or a high opinion of himself, for the share he had in the restoring of his hand? Yet our share in the raising up of the spiritual life within us is the same. All that we can do by our own activity is only like this man's stretching out his hand; the rest is the work of Christ, the only Giver of life to the withered hand or the dead soul. We can only do living works when we are so far born again as to be able to say with the apostle, *"Yet not I, but Christ* [who] *liveth in me"* (Gal. 2:20).

OUR ABSOLUTE DEPENDENCE UPON GOD

Now I will further show how the person who feels the call of God to repentance is to behave under it so that this stirring of the divine power in the soul may have its full effect and bring forth the birth of the new man in Christ Jesus. We are to consider it— as the truth it is—as the seed of the divine nature within us that can only grow by its own strength and its union with God. It is a divine life and therefore can grow from nothing but divine power.

The Virgin Mary's contribution to the birth of the holy Jesus was only this single act of faith and resignation to God: *"Behold the handmaid of the Lord; be it unto me according to thy word"* (Luke 1:38). This is all that we can do toward the realization of that new man who is to be born in ourselves. Now this truth is easily consented to, and a man thinks he believes it because he consents to it, or rather, does not deny it. But this is not enough; it is to be understood in a deep, full, and practical assurance, in the same manner as a man knows and believes that he did not create the stars or cause life to rise in himself. And then it is a belief that puts the soul into a right state, that makes room for the operation of God upon it. His light then enters with full power into the soul, and His Holy Spirit moves and directs all that is done in it. So man lives again in God as a new creature.

THE EFFECTS OF THIS ABSOLUTE DEPENDENCE UPON GOD

When this truth is thus firmly believed, it will have these two excellent effects.

First, it will keep the soul fixed and continually turned toward God in faith, prayer, desire, confidence, and yieldedness to Him for all that it wants to have done in it. This will be a continual source of all divine virtues and graces. The individual thus turned to God must be always receiving from Him. He stands at the true door of all divine communications, and the light of God as freely enters into it as the light of the sun enters into the air.

Secondly, it will fix and ground the person in a true and lasting self-denial. By thus knowing and acknowledging our own nothingness and incapacity for good except that of receiving it from God alone, self is wholly denied; its kingdom is destroyed. There is no room left for spiritual pride and self-glorification. We are saved from a holiness like that of the Pharisees, from wrong opinions of our own works and good deeds, and from a multitude of errors. The most dangerous enemies to our souls are those that arise from things that we take ourselves to be either in nature or grace.

But when we once understand, in some good degree, the all of God and the nothingness of ourselves, we have grasped a truth whose usefulness and benefit no words can express. It brings a kind of infallibility into the soul in which it dwells; all that is vain, false, and deceitful is forced to vanish. When our religion is founded on this rock, it has the firmness of a rock, and its height reaches to heaven. The world, the flesh, and the Devil can do no harm to it. All enemies are known, and all are disarmed by this great truth dwelling in our souls.

It is the knowledge of the all of God that makes the cherubim and the seraphim to be flames of divine love. Where this all of God is truly known and felt in any man, there his whole breath and spirit are a fire of love. Nothing but a pure, disinterested love can rise in it, or come from it. It is a love that begins and ends in God. And where this love is born in any creature, there an angelic life is born along with it. This pure love introduces the creature into the all of God. All that is in God is opened in the creature; it is united with God and has the life of God manifested in it.

There is only one salvation for all mankind, and that is the life of God in the soul. God has only one plan or intention toward all mankind, and that is to introduce or generate His own life, light, and Spirit in them, so that every one of them may be like so many images, temples, and habitations of the Holy Trinity.

THE WAY TO THE ONE SALVATION

Now there is only one possible way for man to attain this salvation, or life of God in the soul. There is not one way for a Jew, another for a Christian, and a third for a heathen. No, God is one, human nature is one, salvation is one, and the way to salvation is one; and that way is the desire of the soul turned to God. When this desire is alive and breaks forth in any creature under heaven, then the lost sheep is found, and the Shepherd has it upon His shoulders. Through this desire, the poor Prodigal Son leaves his husks and swine and hurries to his father. It is because of this desire that the father sees the son, while yet afar off, and runs out to meet him, falls on his neck, and kisses him (Luke 15:20).

See here how plainly we are taught that no sooner is this desire arisen and in motion toward God than the operation of God's Spirit answers it and cherishes and welcomes its first beginnings. This is signified by the father's seeing and having compassion on his son while he is yet afar off, that is, in the first beginnings of his desire. In the same way, this desire does all in the matter of salvation. It brings the soul to God, and God into the soul. It unites with God, it cooperates with God, and it is one life with God.

Oh, my God, just and good, how great is Your love and mercy to mankind, that heaven is thus everywhere open, and Christ is thus the common Savior to all who turn the desire of their hearts to You! O holy Jesus, heavenly light, who lights every man who comes into the world (John 1:9), who redeems every soul who follows Your light, which is always within him! O Holy Trinity, immense ocean of divine love in which all mankind live, and move, and have their being! (See Acts 17:28.) None are separated from You; none live outside of Your love; but all are embraced in the arms of Your mercy. All are partakers of Your divine life, the operation of Your Holy Spirit, as soon as their hearts are turned to You.

This is the plain and easy and simple way of salvation, needing no skills or methods, no borrowed learning, no cultivation of reason, but all done by the simple, natural motion of every heart that truly longs for God. For no sooner is the finite desire of man in motion toward God than the infinite desire of God is united with him and cooperates with him. And in this united desire of God and the creature is the salvation and life of the soul brought forth. For the soul is shut out of God and imprisoned in its own dark workings of flesh and blood, merely and solely because it desires to live for the vanity of this world. This desire is its darkness, its death, its imprisonment, and its separation from God.

The One Way of Salvation

When, therefore, the first spark of a desire for God arises in your soul, cherish it with all your care. Give all your heart into it; it is nothing less than a touch of the divine magnet that is to draw you out of the vanity of time into the riches of eternity. Get up, therefore, and follow it as gladly as the wise men of the East followed the star from heaven that appeared to them. It will do for you what the star did for them; it will lead you to the birth of Jesus, not in a stable at Bethlehem in Judea, but to the birth of Jesus in the dark center of your own fallen soul.

I will conclude this discussion with the words of the heavenly illuminated and blessed man, the German writer, Jacob Behmen (or Boehme):

> It is much to be lamented that we are so blindly led, and that the truth is withheld from us through imaginary conceptions; for if the divine power in the inward ground of the soul was manifest, and working with its luster in us, then the whole Triune God is present in the life and will of the soul. Heaven, in which God dwells, is opened in the soul; and there, in the soul is the place where the Father brings forth His Son, and where the Holy Spirit proceeds from the Father and the Son.
>
> Christ said, *"I am the light of the world: he that followeth me shall not walk in darkness"* (John 8:12). He directs us only to Himself. He is the Morning Star, and is generated and rises in us, and shines in the darkness of our nature. Oh, how great a triumph is there in the soul when He rises in it! Then a man knows, as he never knew before, that he is a stranger in a foreign land.

God's Power in You

A PRAYER

O heavenly Father, infinite, fathomless depth of never-ceasing love, save me from myself, from the disorderly workings of my fallen, long-corrupted nature, and let my eyes see, my heart and spirit feel and find, Your salvation in Christ Jesus.

O God, who made me for Yourself, to show forth Your goodness in me, I humbly beseech You to manifest the life-giving power of Your holy nature within me; help me to such a true and living faith in You, such strength of hunger and thirst after the birth, life, and Spirit of Your holy Jesus in my soul, that all that is within me may be turned from every inward thought or outward work that is not You, Your holy Jesus, and a heavenly work in my soul. Amen.